P9-DCV-603

LIFE Sixty Years

A 60th Anniversary Celebration

1936–1996

LIFE Sixty Years
A 60th Anniversary Celebration
1936 – 1996

EDITOR: Melissa Stanton
DESIGNER: Marti Golon
PICTURE EDITOR: Barbara Baker Burrows
WRITER: Allison Adato
ASSISTANT PICTURE EDITORS: Patricia Cadley, Samantha Hoyt, Lynne Jaeger Weinstein
ASSISTANT EDITOR: Harriet Barovick
COPY EDITOR: Nikki Amdur
ASSISTANT MANAGING EDITOR: Susan Bolotin
DIRECTOR OF DESIGN: Tom Bentkowski
ADDITIONAL STAFF: Robert Friedman (editing); Stanley Mieses (writing);
Priya Giri, Romy Pokorny (research); Melanie deForest (pictures);
Kathleen Berger, Barbara Mead, Christine McNulty, Larry Nesbitt, Michael L. Ronall (copy);
Steve Walkowiak, Michael Gros (technology)

Time Inc. New Business Development
DIRECTOR: David Gitow
ASSOCIATE DIRECTOR: Stuart Hotchkiss
ASSISTANT DIRECTOR: Peter Shapiro
FULFILLMENT MANAGER: Michele Gudema
DEVELOPMENT MANAGERS: Robert Fox, Michael Holahan, John Sandklev, Alicia Wilcox
EDITORIAL OPERATIONS MANAGER: John Calvano
PRODUCTION MANAGER: Donna Miano-Ferrara
FINANCIAL MANAGER: Tricia Griffin
ASSOCIATE DEVELOPMENT MANAGERS: Ken Katzman, Daniel Melore,
Allison Weiss, Dawn Weland
ASSISTANT DEVELOPMENT MANAGER: Charlotte Siddiqui
MARKETING ASSISTANT: Lyndsay Jenks

PICTURE SOURCES are listed by page. 67: © Halsman Estate. 82: W. Eugene Smith/Black Star. 84, 86: © Halsman Estate. 89: bottom left, © 1996 The Archives of Milton H. Greene, L.L.C.. 110: W. Eugene Smith/Black Star. 111: © Halsman Estate. 139: W. Eugene Smith/Black Star. 146: bottom left, © 1996 Long Photo. 166: top left, © 1994 Barbara Morgan/Willard & Barbara Morgan Archive/Time Inc. is the Licensee. 168: © Halsman Estate. 180-181: © 1981 Center for Creative Photography, Arizona Board of Regents.

Published by

Books
Time Inc.
1271 Avenue of the Americas
New York, New York, 10020

Distributed by
Bulfinch Press,
an imprint and trademark of
Little, Brown and Company (Inc.)
Boston • New York • Toronto • London

First Edition
ISBN 0-8212-2335-6
Library of Congress Catalog Card Number 96-85949
"LIFE" is a registered trademark of Time Inc.

PRINTED IN THE UNITED STATES OF AMERICA

BY THE EDITORS OF LIFE

LIFE Sixty Years

A 60TH ANNIVERSARY CELEBRATION 1936–1996

60th Anniver

ISSUE NO. 1

The first issue of LIFE (left) was dated November 23, 1936. The magazine's mission, largely inspired—or at least made possible—by the invention of the portable 35mm camera, was, as set forth by founder Henry R. Luce, "to see life; to see the world." And what a world it was: The United States was in the midst of the Depression, Hitler had recently formed his Axis alliance with Mussolini, Spain was torn by civil war, FDR had just been elected to a second term, and Helen Hayes was conquering Broadway.

While it is unnecessary to say that the world has changed in the last 60 years, it is still fascinating to see how great the transformation has been. And that is our mission in this book—to see the world not just as it is but as it has been during the past six decades. We started by looking through the more than 2,100 issues of LIFE that have appeared so far: thousands upon thousands upon thousands of images. And then, since even more of the past is preserved in LIFE's picture collection—the home for millions of photographs, most rarely or never seen in print—we went there, too. Who better than we to appreciate the fallibility of editors? We know firsthand that for almost every photograph published in LIFE, an equally good image is left behind on the darkroom floor. Several such photos are making their LIFE debut here. Among them: Alfred Eisenstaedt's portrait of Marilyn Monroe (page 84) and Larry Burrows's photograph of wounded soldiers in Vietnam (page 60). We likewise know that photographs are often not published until years after they are taken; sometimes they are considered not historically significant, sometimes *too* significant. We also looked for those pictures, ones like the photograph of the atom bomb being dropped on Nagasaki (page 96). That's why each caption refers to the year the photograph was taken, not to when it first appeared.

But all this is detail. What matters in the end is the richness of the experience. Not as comprehensive history (which is why you won't find every classic image, every significant person or event here), but as life—as it has been lived, decade by decade. By you. By us. And by LIFE.—*The Editors of* LIFE

sary

60TH ANNIVERSARY

LIFE

ISSUE NO. 2,128

AQUACADE CHAMPIONSHIPS
SILVER SPRINGS, FLA., 1953

PHILIPPE HALSMAN

PATRICK LICHFIELD/CAMERA PRESS-RETNA LTD.

QUEEN ELIZABETH AND HER NEW DAUGHTER-IN-LAW, DIANA, PREPARE TO GREET THE PUBLIC. BUCKINGHAM PALACE, JULY 29, 1981

GEORGE SILK

THE PIRATES WIN THE WORLD SERIES.
PITTSBURGH, OCTOBER 13, 1960

GREEN VINE SNAKE
LA SELVA, COSTA RICA, 1982

MICHAEL MELFORD

SEGREGATION
MOBILE, ALA.,1956

PLASTIC FOOD KEEPER
DAIRY QUEEN
Butter Pecan

OOT LON
HOT DOG

ASH RAINS DOWN AFTER THE
ERUPTION OF MOUNT PINATUBO.
LUZON ISLAND, THE PHILIPPINES, 1991

PHILIPPE BOURSEILLER/HOA-QUI

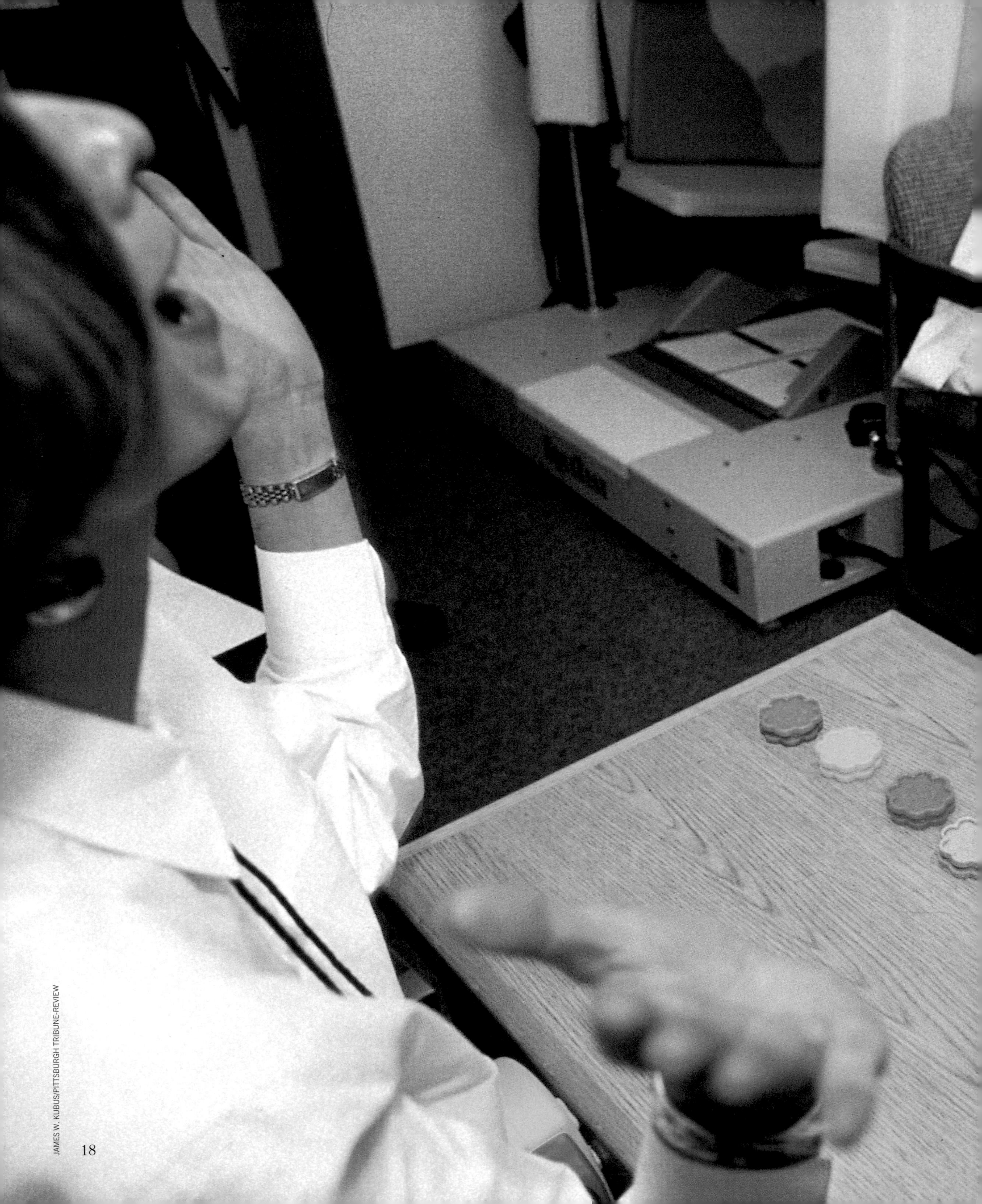

JAMES W. KUBUS/PITTSBURGH TRIBUNE-REVIEW

A DEAF CHILD HEARS FOR THE FIRST TIME. PITTSBURGH, 1993

White

MAMIE AND DWIGHT D. EISENHOWER 11/17/52

“At night, before we'd go to sleep, Jack liked to play some records; and the song he loved most came at the very end of this record. The lines he loved to hear were: *Don't let it be forgot, that once there was a spot, for one brief shining moment that was known as Camelot.* There'll be great Presidents again ... but **THERE'LL NEVER BE ANOTHER CAMELOT** again.”

—JACQUELINE KENNEDY, IN AN INTERVIEW WITH LIFE ONE WEEK AFTER HER HUSBAND'S ASSASSINATION LIFE, DECEMBER 6, 1963

House

TRUMAN'S WACKY WARDROBE 12/10/51

JACQUELINE KENNEDY 9/1/61

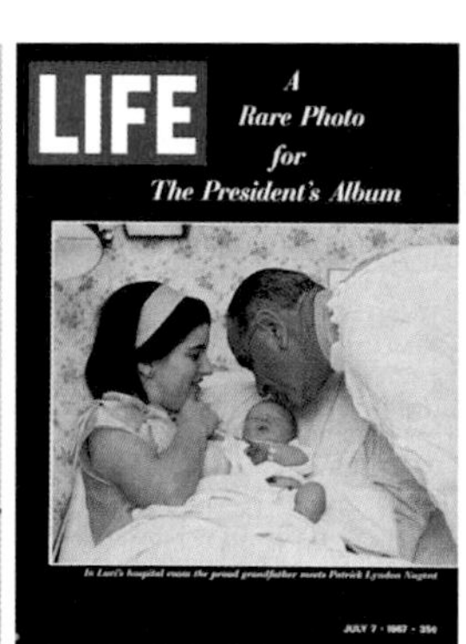

LBJ AND FAMILY 7/7/67

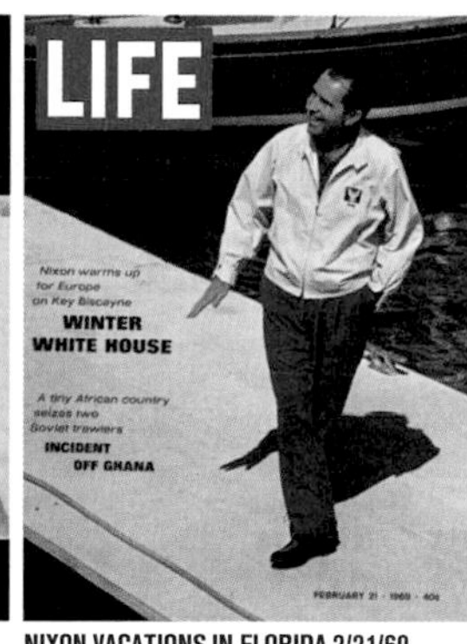

NIXON VACATIONS IN FLORIDA 2/21/69

REAGAN ON HIS RANCH 5/81

THE FIRST LADY AND FIRST PUPS 5/89

From FDR to Bill Clinton, LIFE has known 11 Presidents, documenting their political and personal dramas, as well as those of their families—before, during and after their stays in the White House. While every President, and every First Lady, has shown up on LIFE's cover, the magazine has had its favorites. John and Jacqueline Kennedy hold the record: She has been on 26 covers; he on 25. The runner-up: Ike, with 20. While Presidents Ford, Carter, Bush and Clinton have made only small, cameo cover appearances, First Lady Barbara Bush and First Dog Millie (and her puppies) got star billing (above). LBJ's beagles made the cover too, as did JFK Jr.'s first birthday and the White House weddings of First Daughters Luci Johnson and Tricia Nixon. Another milestone: The only time LIFE's red logo was printed in black was in honor of President Kennedy, after his assassination.

60

Elected by a Depression-weary nation, Franklin Delano Roosevelt gave America a New Deal—and courage during war.

THOMAS MCAVOY

▲ THE FIRST LADY AT A PARTY SHE THREW FOR ARMY TROOPS, JUNE 1942

▼ WINSTON CHURCHILL, FDR AND JOSEPH STALIN, YALTA CONFERENCE, FEBRUARY 1945

U.S. ARMY PHOTOGRAPH

He was the first President to appear in LIFE, which made its debut 16 days after his election to a second term. Franklin Roosevelt and his wife, Eleanor, had a knack for setting precedents. FDR was the first President to appoint a woman to the Cabinet (Labor Secretary Frances Perkins), host a black head of state (Edwin Barclay of Liberia) and appear on television (in a broadcast from the 1939 World's Fair); he was also the first President whose mother had the right to vote. Eleanor Roosevelt was the first White House wife to travel abroad in an airplane (to the Caribbean, in 1934), hold her own press conferences and play a significant public role beyond that of First Hostess; she traveled where the polio-crippled FDR couldn't, visiting coal miners in tunnels and soldiers in the field. He created social security, led America out of the Depression and through World War II. She wrote a newspaper column and lobbied for social programs. FDR, the first President to be elected to a third and fourth term, died in office on April 12, 1945, a month before Germany's surrender. He was 63. LIFE, a frequent critic, eulogized him as a "gallant, fearless man, who could not stand on his own feet without help, [but] bestrode his country like a giant."

MARIE HANSEN

ADDRESSING THE NATION FROM THE WHITE HOUSE IN A "FIRESIDE CHAT" THE NIGHT BEFORE D-DAY, JUNE 5, 1944

"Give 'em hell, Harry" was the rallying cry of his supporters; his critics countered with "to err is **Truman**."

SNIFFING FLOWERS ON THE WHITE HOUSE GROUNDS, 1946

ASSOCIATED PRESS (2)

After the U.S. dropped two atomic bombs on Japan, ending World War II, Harry Truman asked of his country, "Let us use that force and all our resources and all our skills in the great cause of a just and lasting peace." But in his second term America was at war again, in Korea. In the interim, the Democrat from Independence, Mo., set the U.S. on the course of containing communism worldwide, signed the NATO pact and made early civil rights strides by desegregating the armed forces. His wife, Bess, unlike her predecessor, kept to herself and stuck close to the White House. ("I'm not going down any coal mines," she declared.) Harry, however, found the place confining, calling it a "great white prison."

▼ THE PRESIDENT AND FIRST LADY AT THE ARMY-NAVY GAME, PHILADELPHIA, NOVEMBER 26, 1949

Even Democrat Adlai Stevenson, defeated twice by five-star general Dwight D. Eisenhower, said, "I like Ike too."

UPI/CORBIS/BETTMANN

▲ THE FIRST COUPLE AND VICE PRESIDENT RICHARD NIXON AND HIS WIFE, PAT, CELEBRATE IKE'S REELECTION, WASHINGTON, D.C., NOVEMBER 6, 1956.

He golfed. His wife, Mamie, was the perfect hostess. And he had won the war in Europe. No wonder so many people liked Ike. LIFE was especially fond of the Republican President, endorsing him twice. (In 1953, Eisenhower named Clare Boothe Luce, wife of editor-in-chief Henry Luce, ambassador to Italy.) But not everyone found Ike likable. He did not favor the Supreme Court's school desegregation decision, and in 1957, when Arkansas National Guardsmen blocked nine black children from entering a Little Rock school, he waited 20 days before sending in federal troops to enforce the law. On other fronts, he finalized a truce to end the Korean War, warned against what he called the growing "military-industrial complex," and, in a 1963 draft of his memoirs, wrote, "The jungles of Indochina . . . would have swallowed up division after division of United States troops." He omitted the passage before publication because of U.S. involvement in Vietnam under Lyndon Johnson. A West Point man, Ike remained loyal to the commander in chief.

John Fitzgerald **Kennedy** brought elegance and youth to the White House. A thousand days later he was gone.

■ SENATOR AND MRS. KENNEDY WITH DAUGHTER CAROLINE, HYANNIS PORT, MASS., 1959

▶ JFK (LEFT) AND BROTHER ROBERT, THEN HIS CAMPAIGN MANAGER, LATER HIS ATTORNEY GENERAL, LOS ANGELES, JULY 1960

The torch has been passed to a new generation," said the first President born in the 20th century. He was 43, his wife 31. But LIFE's fascination with the new First Family had begun long before. JFK and his eight siblings first appeared in LIFE in 1937, when their father, Joe, was ambassador to Britain. And the magazine was the first to put Jackie on its cover (in 1953, after she and Kennedy became engaged). As President, JFK created the Peace Corps and, after weathering several cold war crises, signed the Nuclear Test Ban Treaty. It all ended on November 22, 1963, in a car, LIFE wrote, "full of blood and red roses." After interviewing the bereaved First Lady, the magazine dubbed the Kennedy era Camelot.

CHATTING WITH WEST VIRGINIA COAL MINERS DURING THE PRESIDENTIAL CAMPAIGN, APRIL 1960

He promised a Great Society, but Lyndon Baines Johnson presided over a divided nation.

▲ LBJ AND LADY BIRD SHARE A QUIET MOMENT AT THE WHITE HOUSE, 1965.

Sworn in on Air Force One beside a bloodied Jacqueline Kennedy, Lyndon Johnson ended his presidency on a low note as well, declining to run for reelection in 1968. He initiated a progressive program of social welfare reforms, but the Texan's administration was plagued by race riots and an ever escalating Vietnam war. His wife, Lady Bird, tried to focus on more positive concerns, advocating for National Parks and for the beautification of Washington, D.C., and the nation's highways. Still, daughter Luci has said the first words she heard when waking at the White House were often those of protesters shouting, "Hey, hey, LBJ, how many kids did you kill today?"

YOICHI OKAMOTO (2)

THE PRESIDENT AND GRANDSON PATRICK LYNDON NUGENT, 1, PLAY COWBOY, THE WHITE HOUSE, JUNE 1968.

DELAWARE
FORNIA
I LIKE
IKE

He lived many political lives, but Richard M. Nixon will be known forever as the first American President to resign from office.

◀ SENATOR AND PAT NIXON AFTER HIS NOMINATION AS IKE'S RUNNING MATE, REPUBLICAN NATIONAL CONVENTION, CHICAGO, JULY 1952

▼ PRESIDENT NIXON AT A DINNER HOSTED BY CHINESE PREMIER CHOU EN-LAI (SECOND FROM LEFT), HANGCHOW, FEBRUARY 1972

Nearly a decade after his supposed political death—losing the 1960 presidential election and, two years later, a bid for the California governorship—Richard Nixon moved into the White House. The consummate cold warrior, he surprised his political foes by establishing relations with Red China and traveling to Moscow, where he began arms-control talks with Leonid Brezhnev. But he also widened the war in Vietnam, before withdrawing troops in 1973. Nixon's true political death came when he was implicated in a 1972 break-in, by his campaign operatives, of Democratic party headquarters in the Watergate hotel. The theme of Nixon's second inaugural parade had been "The Spirit of '76." Having resigned the presidency on August 9, 1974, he spent the bicentennial in exile at his home in San Clemente, Calif.

▶ NIXON AND DAUGHTER TRICIA REHEARSE ON THE EVE OF HER WEDDING, WHITE HOUSE ROSE GARDEN, JUNE 11, 1971.

HARRY BENSON

OLLIE ATKINS/THE WHITE HOUSE

RALPH MORSE

Chosen by one man but rejected by voters, Gerald Ford was a half-term President.

DAVID HUME KENNERLY/THE WHITE HOUSE

▲ WHILE THE FIRST LADY RECOVERED FROM A MASTECTOMY, DAUGHTER SUSAN ACCOMPANIED THE PRESIDENT TO A RECEPTION AT THE WHITE HOUSE, OCTOBER 1974.

BOB DAUGHERTY/ASSOCIATED PRESS

▲ PRESIDENT CARTER TAKES TO THE ROAD, BARDSTOWN, KY., JULY 1979.

"I assume the presidency under extraordinary circumstances never before experienced by Americans," said Gerald Ford after his swearing-in. A month later he pardoned Nixon; the following spring he ordered the airlift evacuation of the U.S. embassy in Saigon when South Vietnam fell to the communists. During his brief tenure he survived two assassination attempts. His wife, Betty, distinguished herself by speaking frankly about her personal battles with breast cancer and, later, drug and alcohol addiction.

A down-to-earth man from Plains, Ga., Jimmy Carter told it straight; too often the news was bad.

He came to Washington with a peanut farmer's good sense—he was the first President to walk to the White House after his inauguration. During the energy crisis, Jimmy Carter told the public to lower their thermostats. His soft-spoken manner helped him coax Israel and Egypt to make peace. But when he failed to free Americans held hostage in Iran, a weary Carter came to mirror a nation's malaise. An upbeat Republican from California named Ronald Reagan sent the Democrat and his wife, Rosalynn, back to Georgia.

Like the movie hero he once was, Ronald **Reagan** took a would-be assassin's bullet—and barely winced.

DAVID BURNETT/CONTACT PRESS

▲ REAGAN AND SOVIET LEADER MIKHAIL GORBACHEV, GENEVA SUMMIT, NOVEMBER 1985

▼ A MONTH BEFORE THE ATTEMPT ON HIS LIFE, REAGAN CUT IN ON NANCY'S DANCE WITH FRANK SINATRA, FEBRUARY 6, 1981.

The first First Couple with movie credits, Ronald and Nancy Reagan brought Hollywood glamour and showmanship to the White House. His vision of an America strengthened by supply-side economics appealed to many, as did his call for a return to traditional family values. Reagan built up an arsenal of high-tech weaponry, and his relations with the U.S.S.R. had the good-versus-evil feel of a western, but he later made a friend of Mikhail Gorbachev, with whom he signed a nuclear-arms-reduction treaty. When the Iran-contra scandal involving covert arms sales erupted during his second term, and critics questioned whether the nation's oldest President (69 when he took office) was too old for the job, he never faltered. Opinion polls showed Ronald Reagan to be the most popular President since FDR.

MICHAEL EVANS/THE WHITE HOUSE

BEN WEAVER

NANCY REAGAN GREETS HER HUSBAND (WAVING FROM HIS HOTEL ROOM), DURING HER APPEARANCE AT THE REPUBLICAN NATIONAL CONVENTION, DALLAS, AUGUST 22, 1984.

After eight years as Reagan's VP, George **Bush**, a former U.S. envoy to China and CIA director, got the keys to the White House.

DAVID VALDEZ/THE WHITE HOUSE

The cold war ended on his watch, but George Bush had other battles to fight. He sent U.S. troops to Panama (to oust its leader, Gen. Manuel Noriega), to Somalia (to aid in famine relief and keep the peace), and, in a massive deployment, to the Persian Gulf to stop the "naked aggression" of Iraq's Saddam Hussein. The gulf war sent Bush's approval ratings soaring, but his polls took a turn for the worse in the fall of 1991, after his nominee to the Supreme Court, conservative Clarence Thomas, was accused of sexual harassment. When Bush ran for reelection in 1992, his loyalty to the GOP's right wing led many moderate voters, particularly women, to look elsewhere.

▲ VICE PRESIDENT AND BARBARA BUSH—AND GRANDKIDS—AT THEIR SUMMER HOME IN KENNEBUNKPORT, MAINE, AUGUST 1987

▶ THE PRESIDENT AND FIRST LADY MAKE A THANKSGIVING VISIT TO U.S. TROOPS IN SAUDI ARABIA, NOVEMBER 1990.

JEAN-LOUIS ATLAN/SYGMA

A saxophone-playing Rhodes scholar and four-term Arkansas governor, Bill **Clinton** became America's first baby boomer President.

DAVID LONGSTREATH/ASSOCIATED PRESS

"Buy one, get one free," quipped Bill Clinton about his partnership with his wife, and fellow lawyer, Hillary Rodham Clinton. When he took office, she took on healthcare reform, but they were unable to get a bill passed. He successfully brokered a peace between the PLO and Israel, and he signed gun-control and family-medical-leave laws that his two predecessors opposed. But alleged improprieties involving Whitewater, a land investment made by the couple, haunted the Clintons. Despite the scrutiny and deadlocks with a Republican Congress, the man from Hope, Ark.—who, as a boy, aspired to political life—kept his enthusiasm for the job.

▲ PRESIDENT-ELECT CLINTON JOINS THE BAND AT A DEMOCRATIC RALLY, MACON, GA., NOVEMBER 23, 1992.

▶ BILL AND HILLARY CLINTON, INAUGURATION GALA, JANUARY 20, 1993

DAVID BURNETT/CONTACT PRESS

“The open kitchen **KEEPS THE HOUSEWIFE IN EASIER TOUCH WITH HER FAMILY** than the enclosed kitchen most builders provide. The family room for television, games, sewing or ironing keeps the living room clean and uncluttered.”

—FROM “$15,000 TRADE SECRETS HOUSE,” A STORY ABOUT EASY-TO-BUILD, PREFABRICATED HOMES LIFE, JANUARY 5, 1953

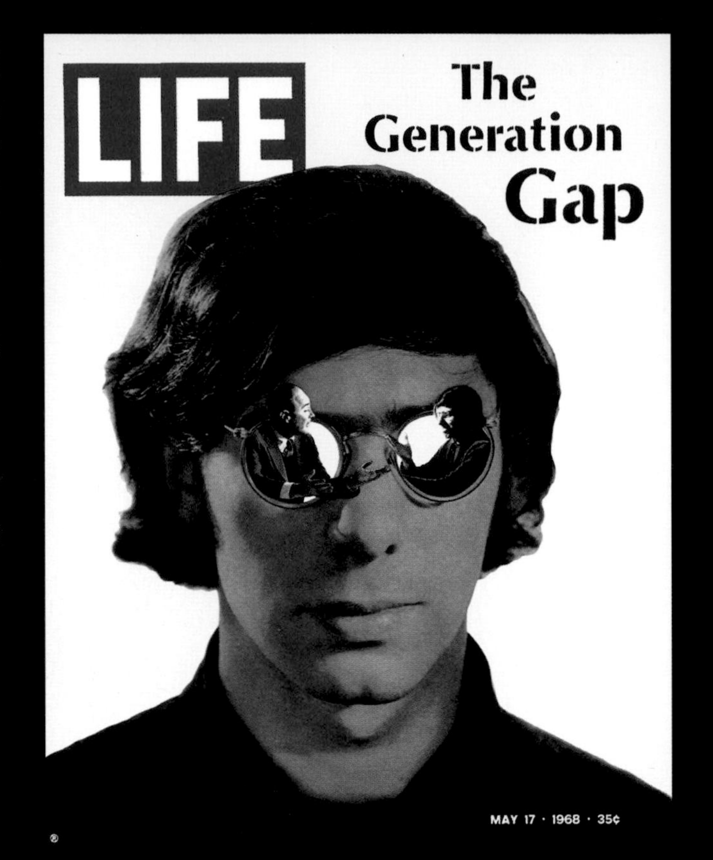

SEPARATE WORLDS 5/17/68

The Way We

Though extraordinary news will always grab the headlines, and paparazzi will always chase the stars, the stuff of everyday life is what often matters most. Going on a date to a drive-in diner (such as to Sivils in Houston, below, far left). Graduating from high school. (Of Forest, Ohio's Class of 1943, LIFE said: "The boys were stiff and uncomfortable in their black gowns and the girls had suddenly changed overnight from jitterbugs in socks and sweaters into poised creatures with an unaccountable dignity.") Working, getting married, buying a home, having babies. (From a 1950 story about pregnancy: "The natural childbirth method is not childbirth by hypnosis; nor is it childbirth without pain or without drugs. It is simply childbirth without fear.") And finally, at the end of a busy day, taking time out for prayer and contemplation.

CARHOP AT A TEXAS DRIVE-IN 2/26/40

HIGH SCHOOL GRADUATION 6/14/43

NATURAL CHILDBIRTH 1/30/50

FAT DAYS IN THE FARM BELT 7/14/58

COLLEGE COHABITATION 11/20/70

HOW AMERICANS PRAY 3/94

Live 60

FENNO JACOBS

Daily life in America could be cheerful, despite the Depression, and peaceful, despite the world war.

NINA LEEN

▶ LEMCKE'S RECORD STORE, WEBSTER GROVES, MO., 1944

◀ NEW YORK CITY, 1937

The harsh realities of the 1930s and early 1940s—the Depression and then a world war—had a way of disappearing off the radar of young Americans, if only during a few moments of fun. On a hot day in the city, a toddler could still delight in the spray of a tapped fire hydrant (left). And, as LIFE reported in 1944, there were "some 6,000,000 teen-age girls . . . in a world all their own . . . [a] blissful society almost untouched by the war." Crooners like Frank Sinatra provided the soundtrack for that dreamy world where girls—and boys—spent hours listening to new releases at their local record shop (above). Adults didn't have as much time for play. With men off at war, women went off to work. LIFE aided their efforts: In a 1943 article, actress Veronica Lake showed female factory workers how to operate a drill press without getting their hair caught.

MARGARET BOURKE-WHITE

▲ FEMALE "BURNERS" BEVEL ARMOR PLATING FOR TANKS, GARY, IND., 1943.

The **postwar years** led to a boom in college enrollment, housing starts, auto sales and, most notably, babies.

YALE JOEL

▶ THE SMITHS, DETROIT, 1954

◀ LITTLE LEAGUERS, MANCHESTER, N.H., 1954

LEONARD MCCOMBE

▲ FRAT BROTHERS SING THE SIGMA CHI "SWEETHEART SONG," WESTMINISTER COLLEGE, FULTON, MO., 1949.

The GI Bill helped returning soldiers go to college—and reorder their lives: In a story about Sigma Chi fraternity houses (including the one at left), LIFE reported that a former Army private had the privilege of hazing his former lieutenant, a new pledge. Veterans could buy a four-room house in Levittown, a newly developed suburb on Long Island, N.Y., for $7,990, no money down. And in Detroit (home of the Smith family, opposite), automakers turned out two million more cars in 1946 than they had the year before. A top seller: the $1,712 Chevrolet station wagon, perfect for the suburban homemaker to shuttle her 2.2 children to and from dance class or Little League (top).

JUN MIKI

Champion

Kids cried, but parents breathed a sigh of relief that protection from polio was just a shot away.

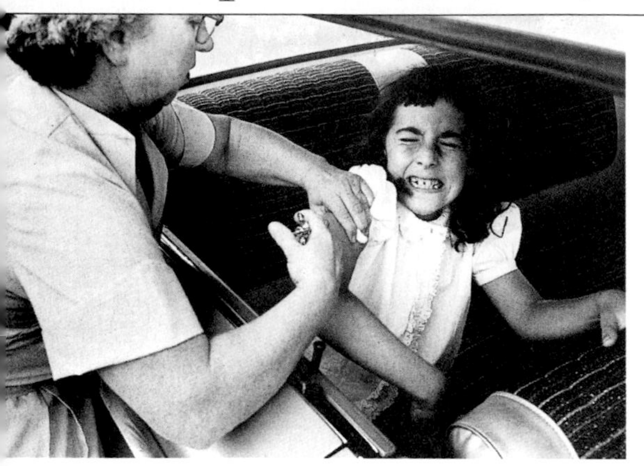

▲ ▶ POLIO VACCINATION DRIVE, GLENDALE, CALIF., 1960

The epidemic, which began early in the century, threatened children—and sometimes adults—with paralysis and death. But the fear of contracting polio, as rampant as the virus itself, subsided practically overnight. On April 12, 1955, immunologist Jonas Salk's vaccine was licensed; it was put to use immediately. Polio cases in the U.S. dropped from 57,897 in 1952 to 5,485 in 1957. Reporting from a drive-in vaccination center (right and above), LIFE noted: "For the children, insulated in their cars against the anguish of customers ahead of them, it was a relatively pleasant and practically painless procedure—except for that brief, inevitable moment when it came their own turn to get stuck."

BILL BRIDGES (2)

JOHN OLSON

Many climbed the corporate ladder. A few dropped out. Some put differences aside and hoped others would too.

HOWARD SOCHUREK

◀ COMMUNE MEMBERS, 1969

▶ MANAGERS MEETING AT IBM, CHICAGO, 1966

▶ INTERRACIAL DATING, UNIVERSITY OF MINNESOTA, 1970

MICHAEL MAUNEY

Even during the era of nonconformity, fitting in with a group was important. In 1966, LIFE went inside computer giant IBM ("a symbol of the faceless technological age") to examine the frustrations of a man striving "for personal achievement in the white-collar world" (above). At the other extreme were people who had dropped out of that world entirely. "They are refugees from affluence," said LIFE of a group of "youthful pioneers" (opposite)—including one former computer programmer—who had set up a commune "somewhere in the woods." (The communers had asked that their location not be revealed.) When members of different groups did choose to mix (left), new divisions arose. Noted the magazine, "The black who decides to go out with a white must face the censure of his own people."

Quick money and credit sent yuppies shopping, but a lack of cash put family farms in the red.

A stifling inflation defined the late 1970s, while materialism—fueled by stock-market killings, Reaganomics and even prime-time TV soaps like *Dallas* and *Dynasty*—drove the 1980s. But in America's heartland, it could have been the 1930s. Export demands had dwindled, land values were falling, the cost of producing a bushel of wheat exceeded its market price, and farmers across the nation were defaulting on their loans. In North Dakota, lawyer Sarah Vogel (far right) worked to save debt-ridden family farms. Others helped too. In 1985 musicians Willie Nelson and John Cougar Mellencamp staged FarmAid, a 14-hour benefit concert in Champaign, Ill. Said singer John Fogerty to the crowd: "The next time you sit down to a very nice meal, remember it didn't come from a cellophane bag from Safeway."

▶ **THE OSTER FARM, WING, N.DAK., 1982**

GREY VILLET

The typical American family c. 1990: often yours, mine and ours

The American family has rarely resembled that of TV's Ozzie and Harriet, the 1950s standard-bearers of marital and parental perfection. Real life is different; real families are different. By 1990, 24 percent of children in the U.S. were living in single-parent households; nearly one in two marriages was ending in divorce. At his father's second marriage, five-year-old Keith Walkowitz (near left) refused to take his place as ring bearer. Two months later his mother remarried.

◀ **BANFIELD-WALKOWITZ WEDDING, FREEHOLD, N.J., 1989**

APRIL SAUL/THE PHILADELPHIA INQUIRER

U.S. AIR FORCE 12/1/41

War

AIR-RAID VICTIM IN ENGLAND 9/23/40

A SOLDIER'S FAREWELL 4/19/43

GEN. DOUGLAS MacARTHUR 8/28/50

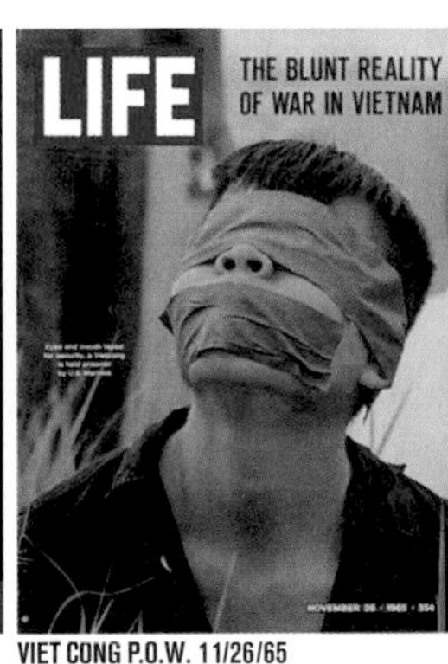

VIET CONG P.O.W. 11/26/65

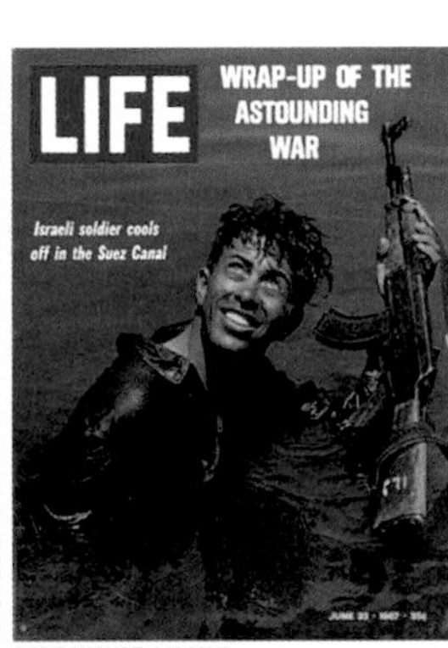

SIX-DAY WAR 6/23/67

PERSIAN GULF WAR 3/91

There has not been a time in LIFE's 60 years when there hasn't been a war somewhere in the world. The magazine made its debut soon after the outbreak of the Spanish civil war; during World War II it was among the first U.S. publications to show photographs of Americans killed in battle. In a quest to document war's toll on individuals—be they young recruits or seasoned officers, prisoners or refugees, widows or orphans—many LIFE photographers have risked their lives. Three were killed: Robert Capa and Larry Burrows in Indochina, Paul Schutzer in Israel during the Six-Day War. LIFE has made its readers feel the pain and loss of wartime tragedies, and in doing so has set a standard of intimacy that has carried through to recent conflicts in the Persian Gulf and Bosnia. Photographs that unblinkingly depict the horror of war remind us how precious peace is.

When the fighting finally ended in 1945, the death count for **World War II** totaled more than 35 million.

W. EUGENE SMITH

▲ BATTLE OF IWO JIMA, 1945

▼ COLOGNE, GERMANY, 1945

JOHNNY FLOREA (2)

When Adolf Hitler invaded Poland in 1939, the world was changed forever. LIFE's photographers witnessed—and recorded—history as it happened. Prussian-born Alfred Eisenstaedt, who fought for Germany during World War I, brought to the magazine behind-the-scenes photos he had taken not only of Hitler but also of Joseph Goebbels and Benito Mussolini. Robert Capa shot pictures as he waded ashore in Normandy on D-Day, dodging bullets alongside Allied troops. Carl Mydans photographed the liberation of a Japanese POW camp in Manila, where he too had been held captive. By the war's end, the world had seen the worst man had to offer: one of the deadliest ground battles of the Pacific front (top left); the despair of 12 million displaced Europeans (left); the Nazi death camps (right) of Hitler's Final Solution; and, in Hiroshima and Nagasaki, the devastating carnage and destruction of the atomic bomb.

▶ NORDHAUSEN, GERMANY, 1945

Peace was still new when fighting began in **Korea**, the first battleground of America's war against communism.

DAVID DOUGLAS DUNCAN (2)

▲ **WOUNDED SOLDIER NEAR THE NAKTONG RIVER, 1950**

▶ **U.S. MARINE, SOUTH KOREA, 1950**

These are "the eyes of men who have looked at undiluted hell," reported LIFE in 1950. Just five years after the jubilation of V-J Day, American troops were fighting to stop the spread of communism into what seemed, to many back home, an insignificant Asian peninsula. America's three frustrating years in Korea defined the limits of what the nation's military could achieve abroad: Its mighty place in the world had changed. David Douglas Duncan, a WW II vet, photographed the brutal tour of a Marine battalion, from combat zones to homesick nights, when dinner was eaten from a frozen tin. "I wanted to show something of the comradeship that binds men together when they are fighting a common peril," said Duncan. That bond is clearly evident in the image (above) of South Korean medics aiding a wounded GI.

PETER LEIBING/CONTI-PRESS FOR AP

In a world divided, the cold war sent a chill of fear through the citizens of both the West and the Eastern bloc.

"An iron curtain has descended across the continent," said Winston Churchill in 1946 about the Soviet-controlled nations of Eastern Europe. With the curtain down, the stage was set for the cold war. In the United States, those fingered as "commie" sympathizers were demonized as traitors, and schoolchildren were taught how to cower under their desks to protect themselves from the blast of The Bomb. The U.S.-Soviet balance of power shifted uneasily—from the botched Bay of Pigs invasion in 1961 to President Kennedy's redemption the following year during the Cuban missile crisis, when the Red Scare came terrifyingly close to home. In East Berlin, in August 1961, a border guard (left) paused briefly at the newly placed barbed-wire fence he was ordered to patrol. Then he fled his post—and his country—by leaping to freedom in the West. After the barbed wire was reinforced by concrete walls and electrical fences, such defections became rare. The Berlin Wall made tangible, and seemingly permanent, the division between West and East, us and them.

◀ **EAST BERLIN, 1961**

The long war in Vietnam tore the U.S. apart—and left more than 58,000 Americans dead.

"More than we must know how many, we must know *who*" were the words that accompanied the shocking photographic roster LIFE ran in the June 27, 1969, issue featuring one week's American dead in Vietnam. The total: 242. Two years later, one fatality was particularly devastating to the magazine's editors. LIFE photojournalist Larry Burrows often said that his greatest wish was to photograph Vietnam at peace. That dream was shot down over Laos while he was flying in a South Vietnamese military helicopter. Burrows was 44. Nearly all the war unfolds in his pictures: from 1962, when the fighting in Vietnam was a small-scale regional conflict, to the United States' deep military involvement; from the haunting faces of civilians to the agony of soldiers who survived battle (right)—or those who did not.

▶ **FIRST-AID STATION NEAR THE DEMILITARIZED ZONE, SOUTH VIETNAM, 1966**

LARRY BURROWS

The arms race was global, but the carnage was local—caused by conventional weapons, genocide and civil war.

ROLAND NEVEU/GAMMA-LIAISON

▲ MASS GRAVE NEAR PHNOM PENH, CAMBODIA, 1981

As the superpowers continued to amass a bloated arsenal of nuclear weapons, the "war" most frequently discussed was the one in which total destruction was mutually assured. The world was spared nuclear annihilation, but not warfare or terror. In the killing fields of Cambodia (above), Pol Pot's Khmer Rouge massacred more than one million people. In El Salvador, military death squads slaughtered civilians and clergy. In Nicaragua, the contras and the Sandinistas battled for power. And in Lebanon (right), civil war turned the once thriving capital of Beirut into a divided city of bombed-out buildings and equally hollow violence.

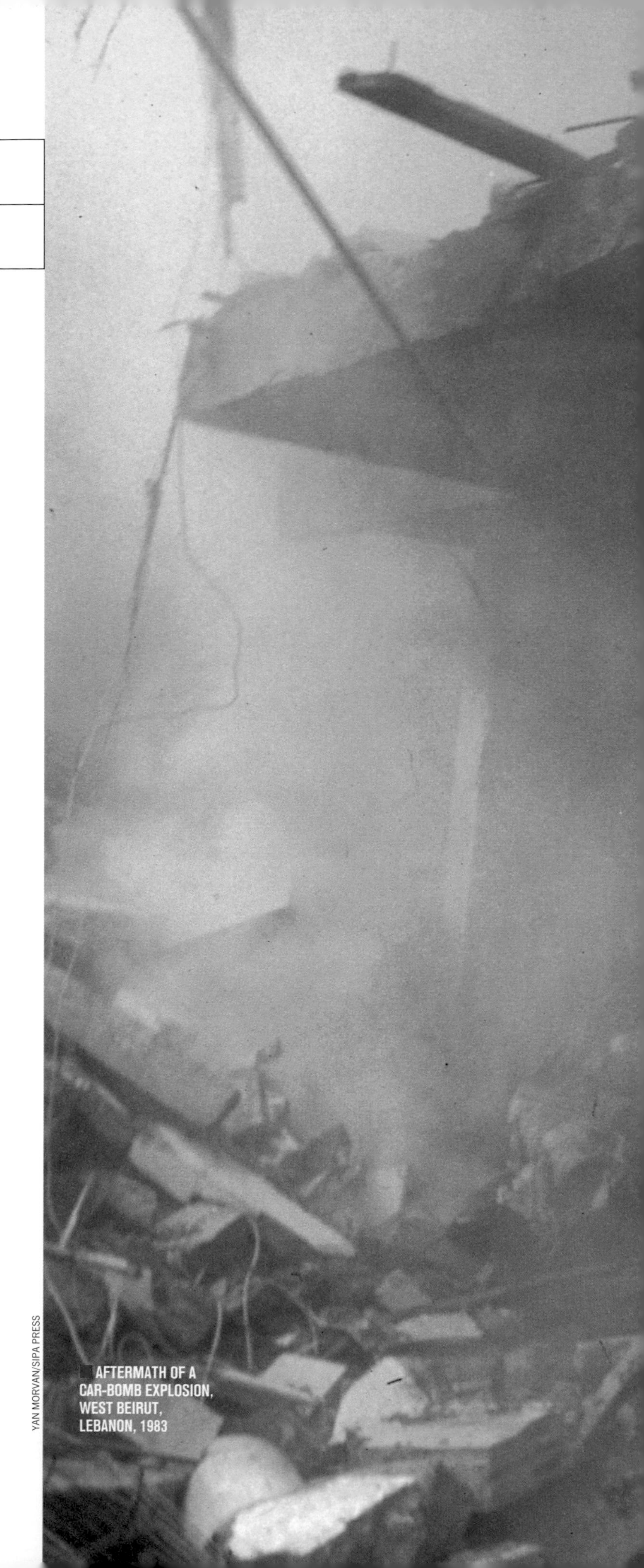

YAN MORVAN/SIPA PRESS

AFTERMATH OF A CAR-BOMB EXPLOSION, WEST BEIRUT, LEBANON, 1983

High-tech and televised around the world, the Persian Gulf war was swift, but long on tragedies.

The Iraqi invasion of Kuwait in August 1990 led to the largest U.S. military deployment in a generation—and, when full-scale war broke out six months later, the first time in 18 years that LIFE appeared in weekly editions. The magazine's schedule was stepped up to cover a war that transfixed television audiences with its nighttime battles resembling the blips and flashes of a Nintendo game. Though critics said the war was being waged to secure America's ties with an oil-rich ally, many in the U.S. were tying yellow ribbons to trees in support of American men and women fighting—and dying—to free Kuwait. Wearing his father's flight jacket, Bennett Edwards, 11 (near right), joined his family in mourning Air Force Capt. Jonathan Edwards, 34, killed while escorting a medevac chopper. Returning troops received a hero's welcome, having removed dictator Saddam Hussein from Kuwait, though not from his rule of Iraq.

► ARLINGTON NATIONAL CEMETERY, VIRGINIA, 1991

MARTIN SIMON-SABA

Celebr

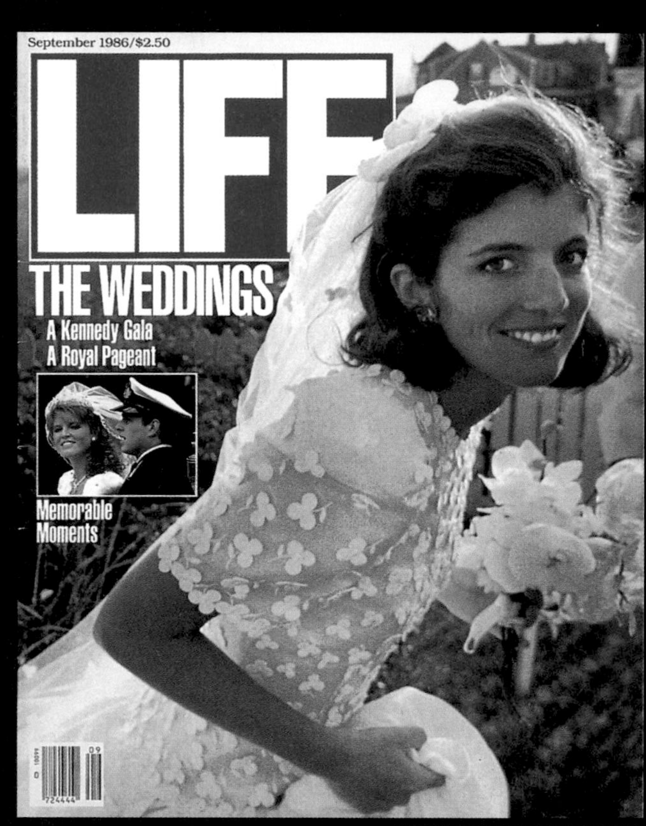
September 1986/$2.50
LIFE
THE WEDDINGS
A Kennedy Gala
A Royal Pageant
Memorable Moments

CAROLINE KENNEDY GETS MARRIED 9/86

“All that energy focused on one performer. And the roar after a song. It was scary. God, **I HAD NEVER SEEN SO MANY PEOPLE.**”

—COUNTRY JOE McDONALD, FOLKSINGER, AT THE WOODSTOCK MUSIC FESTIVAL LIFE, AUGUST 29, 1969

ation

PRE-ELECTION RALLY 11/4/40

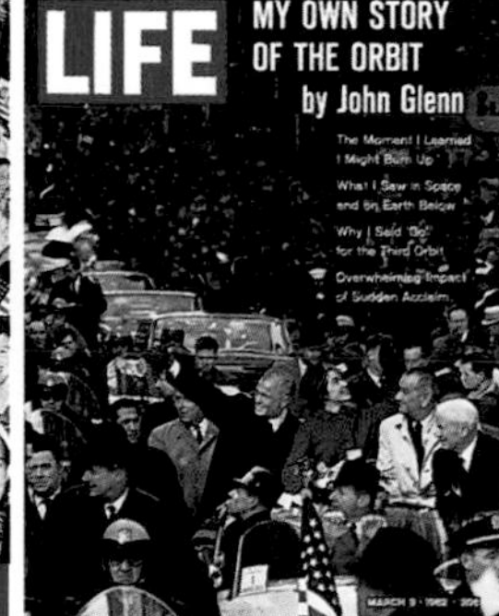

NYC CHEERS JOHN GLENN 3/9/62

A LEGENDARY CONCERT 9/69

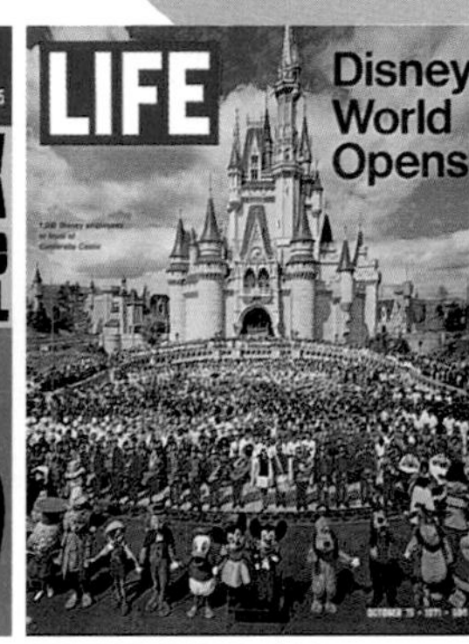

MICKEY'S NEW HOME 10/15/71

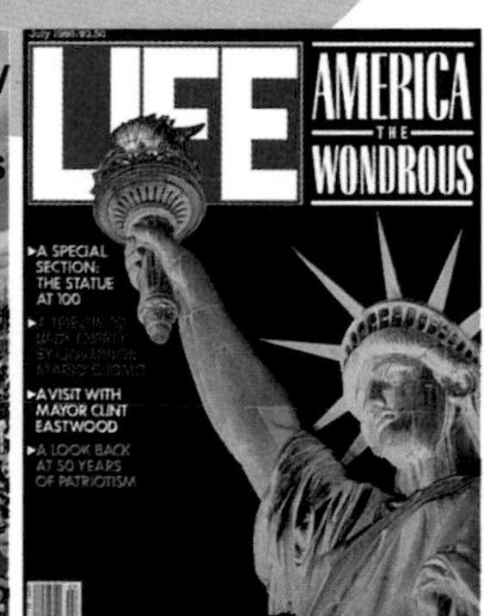

LADY LIBERTY'S 100th BIRTHDAY 7/86

AMERICANS PARTY HEARTY 11/94

Whether it's a global celebration of peace or a holiday barbecue, LIFE rarely misses the chance to play party photographer and, in the process, anthropologist. LIFE was an invited guest at the 1953 wedding of Sen. John F. Kennedy and Jacqueline Bouvier and, 33 years later, at the nuptials of their daughter, Caroline (left), to Edwin Schlossberg. LIFE got soaked at Woodstock—both times—and dressed up for countless debutante balls. And the magazine's photographers have stood among the cheering crowds welcoming astronauts home from space and hostages home from war. So enthusiastically has LIFE worn its party shoes that in 1937 bandleaders Benny Goodman and Harry James honored the magazine with a song. The title: "Life Goes to a Party."

War is over

Three years, eight months and six days after the U.S. entered World War II, the fighting officially ended. President Truman's announcement—at seven p.m. EST on August 14, 1945—that Japan had surrendered started a party that lasted for days. One GI called V-J Day "the kissingest day in history," politely describing the first act of what would soon become the baby boom.

U.S. SERVICEMEN AND SERVICEWOMEN, PARIS, AUGUST 15, 1945

U.S. ARMY PHOTOGRAPH

THE STARS AND STRIPES
PEACE
PEACE
PEACE
PEACE
EXTRA THE STARS AND STRIPES EXTRA
PEACE
EXTRA THE STARS AND STRIPES

Independence Day

In the mid-1950s, when many states were curbing the personal use of fireworks in the interests of public safety, LIFE set off to document what it mistakenly believed was a fast-fading tradition. One enduring image was found on a suburban porch, where four youngsters marked the nation's 178th birthday.

MONROE, WASH., JULY 4, 1954

NAT R. FARBMAN

An American princess

Planning a wedding is nerve-racking for any bride. Grace Kelly planned hers with the world watching. LIFE trailed the Oscar-winning actress as she tended to such prenuptial details as buying shoes, visiting the dentist, packing her trousseau, sailing to Europe with her bridal retinue, and meeting with MGM designer Helen Rose about her taffeta, silk, lace and *peau de soie* wedding gown. LIFE was also there moments before the ceremony in which the 26-year-old Philadelphian wed Prince Rainier III, 32, and became Her Most Serene Highness, Princess Gracia Patricia of Monaco.

MONACO PALACE, APRIL 19, 1956

HOWELL CONANT

Coming home

In early 1973, after the signing of a cease-fire agreement in Paris, 566 American POWs were released by North Vietnam and reunited with their families in the United States. Air Force Lt. Col. Robert Stirm—held captive since 1967—was one of them.

TRAVIS AIR FORCE BASE, CALIF., MARCH 18, 1973

SAL VEDER/AP

Happy 100th!

In 1883 it was a marvel of engineering—the tallest structure in the nation. On its centennial, the Brooklyn Bridge was still an architectural wonder, as well as a busy roadway, carrying 150,000 vehicles a day to and from the boroughs of Brooklyn and Manhattan. Traffic was rerouted the night the East River crossing was feted with a spectacular pyrotechnic bash.

NEW YORK CITY, MAY 24, 1983

HENRY GROSKINSKY

The wall came crumbling down

When East Germany eased travel and emigration restrictions, thousands of East Berliners joined their western neighbors in an impromptu dance atop the barrier that had divided the city for nearly 30 years. Police didn't stop the revelers, even when they jumped down and razed the Berlin Wall with sledgehammers.

EAST BERLIN, NOVEMBER 9, 1989

ALEXANDRA AVAKIAN/WOODFIN CAMP

TOP BOX-OFFICE STAR BETTE DAVIS 1/23/39

Much has changed over the 60 years LIFE has been covering Hollywood—the word "starlet," for instance, has bitten the dust—but much has stayed the same. In LIFE, and in Hollywood, circa 1936 or 1946 or 1956 . . . or 1996, there are heroes: Jimmy Stewart in *Mr. Smith Goes to Washington,* Tom Hanks in *Apollo 13.* There are sirens: Rita Hayworth in *Gilda,* Kathleen Turner in *Body Heat.* There are hoofers: Fred Astaire and Ginger Rogers in *Carefree* (below, far left), Patrick Swayze and Jennifer Grey in *Dirty Dancing.* There are, inevitably, precocious children: Shirley Temple in *Heidi,* Macaulay Culkin in *Home Alone.* There are sequels: Paul Newman in *The Hustler,* Paul Newman in *The Color of Money* (below, far right). And there are, of course, remakes: Laurence Olivier in *Hamlet,* Mel Gibson in *Hamlet.* LIFE has seen them all.

60

GINGER ROGERS AND FRED ASTAIRE 8/22/38

LANA TURNER AND CLARK GABLE 10/13/41

VIVIEN LEIGH & LAURENCE OLIVIER 12/17/51

INGRID BERGMAN 11/26/56

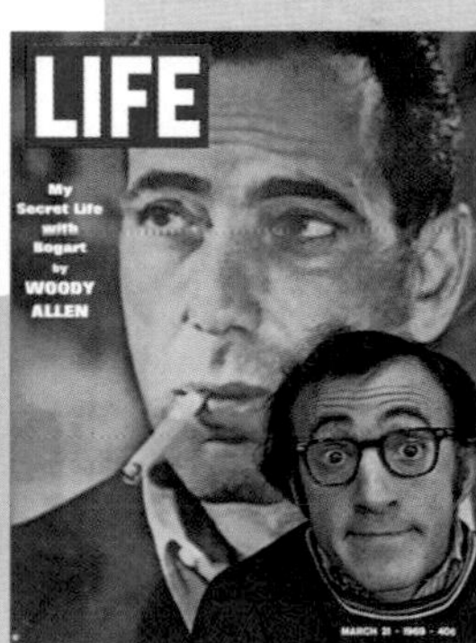

WOODY ON BOGIE 3/21/69

TOM CRUISE AND PAUL NEWMAN 11/86

lywood

ORSON WELLES
CITIZEN KANE
ORSON W
CITIZEN
Its Terrific ORSON WELLES CITIZEN KANE
BELL
20¢ 1ST 1/4 MILE
5¢ EACH ADDL 1/4 MILE

Hepburn . . . Cooper . . . Stewart . . . Grable . . . Welles

ORSON WELLES, 1941

W. EUGENE SMITH

▶ LIFE CALLED KATHARINE HEPBURN, 31, "[A] LANKY, COLTISH THOROUGHBRED" (1939).

▶▶ IN *THE WESTERNER*, GARY COOPER, 39, "DOES ONE OF HIS BEST JOBS AS A WANDERING SADDLE-BUM" (1940).

ALFRED EISENSTAEDT

▶ THE "BOYISH FACE" OF COL. JAMES STEWART, 37, LOOKED "A LITTLE LEANER" AFTER BEING AWAY AT WAR (1945).

▶▶ RISING STAR BETTY GRABLE, 23, KEPT HER FIGURE "BY DANCING IN THE SURF" (1940).

PETER STACKPOLE (3)

He is, by quick turns, an amazingly wise adult and a petulant little boy," said LIFE of Orson Welles in 1941. *Citizen Kane*, the 26-year-old actor-director's film debut, was a masterpiece of cinematography and movie-making. It also did well at the box office. In fact, Welles sometimes checked ticket sales himself—which is what he was about to do at New York's Palace Theater (left).

Taylor . . . Peck . . . Dean . . . Monroe . . . Brando

PHILIPPE HALSMAN

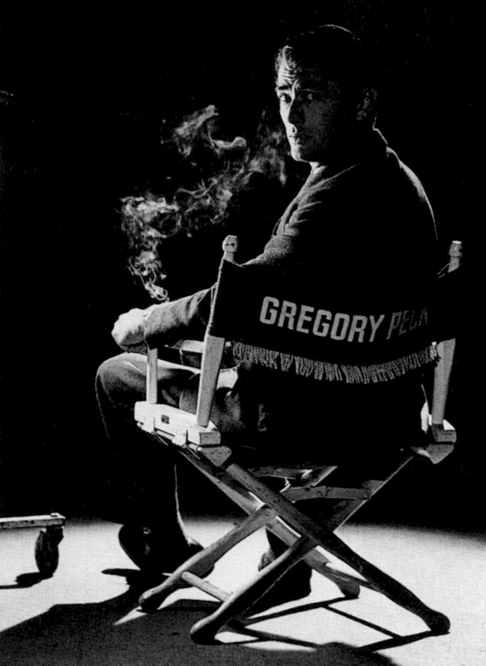

ALLAN GRANT

◀◀ ELIZABETH TAYLOR HAS SAID OF PHILIPPE HALSMAN, WHO TOOK THIS PORTRAIT IN 1948, WHEN SHE WAS JUST 16: "[HE] TAUGHT ME TO USE MY FACE AND BODY."

◀ GREGORY PECK'S "SMOOTH MASCULINE APPEAL IS LEGALLY INCORPORATED," REPORTED LIFE IN 1957, WHEN THE 39-YEAR-OLD ACTOR FORMED HIS OWN PRODUCTION COMPANY.

DENNIS STOCK/MAGNUM PHOTOS

ALFRED EISENSTAEDT

◀◀ JAMES DEAN, 24, "HAS ALWAYS LIKED ANIMALS," LIFE WROTE IN 1955, "BECAUSE, HE SAYS, THEY ACCEPT HIM ON HIS OWN TERMS."

◀ MARILYN MONROE, 1953

Marilyn Monroe first appeared in LIFE in 1949 when she and seven other "starlets" were asked to demonstrate their acting ability. (One assignment: Feign seeing a monster.) The only actress of the bunch to return to LIFE, Monroe has been on the cover 13 times. (Elizabeth Taylor is the only movie star with more: 14.) In a 1962 interview, Monroe, 36, reflected on her fame: "Everybody is always tugging at you. . . . They kind of like take pieces out of you." She died a week after the article was published.

JOHN ENGSTEAD

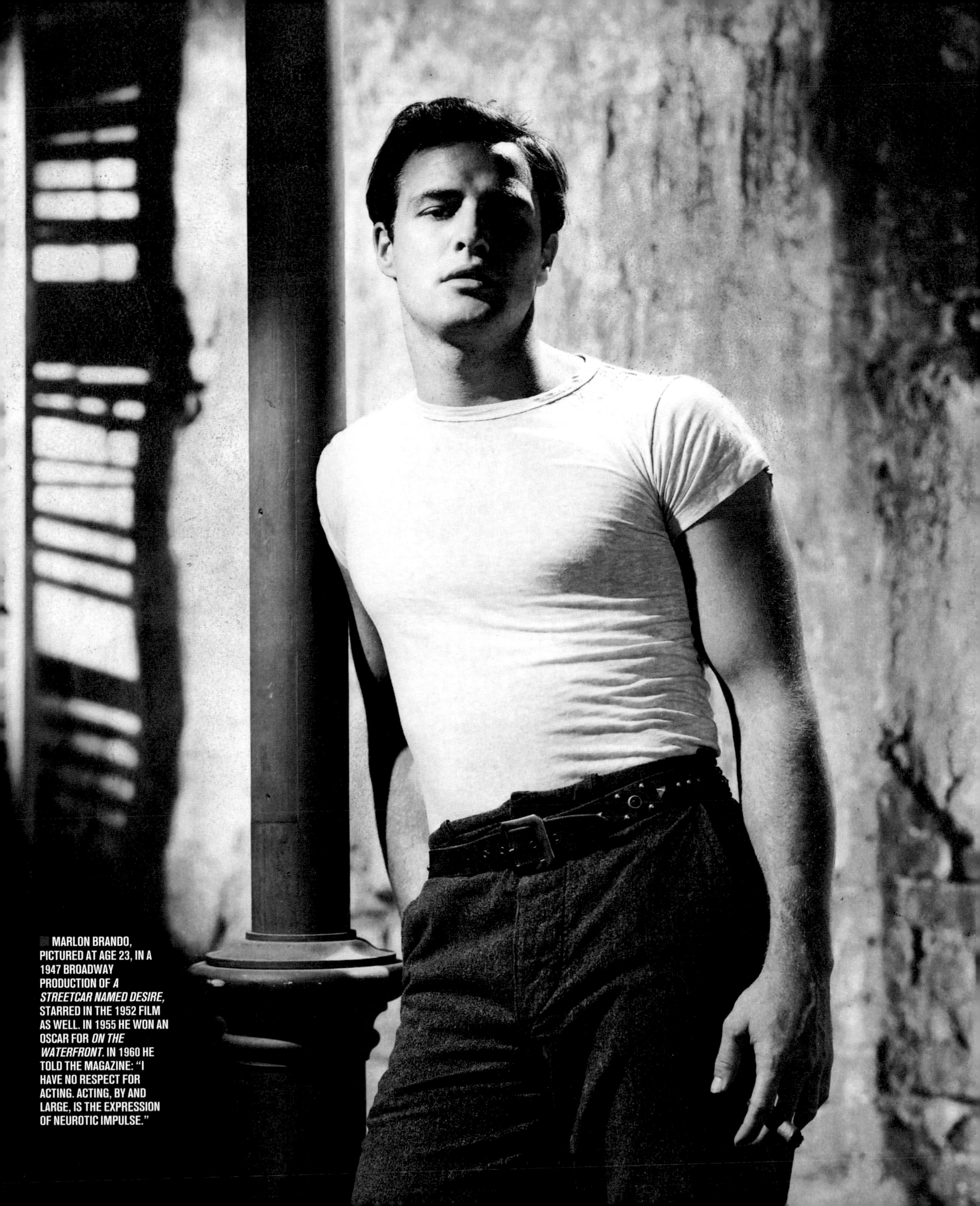

MARLON BRANDO, PICTURED AT AGE 23, IN A 1947 BROADWAY PRODUCTION OF *A STREETCAR NAMED DESIRE,* STARRED IN THE 1952 FILM AS WELL. IN 1955 HE WON AN OSCAR FOR *ON THE WATERFRONT.* IN 1960 HE TOLD THE MAGAZINE: "I HAVE NO RESPECT FOR ACTING. ACTING, BY AND LARGE, IS THE EXPRESSION OF NEUROTIC IMPULSE."

MacLaine . . . Hepburn . . . Wayne . . . Wood . . . Loren

GJON MILI

◀ SHIRLEY MACLAINE HAS HAD AS MANY LIVES ONSCREEN AS SHE CLAIMS TO HAVE HAD IN HER OWN PAST. IN 1963'S *IRMA LA DOUCE*, THE 29-YEAR-OLD ACTRESS WAS A PROSTITUTE.

▼ ABOUT AUDREY HEPBURN (LEAPING IN 1959, AT AGE 30), DIRECTOR BILLY WILDER SAID: "SHE GIVES THE DISTINCT IMPRESSION THAT SHE CAN SPELL 'SCHIZOPHRENIA.'"

PHILIPPE HALSMAN

Sophia Loren was LIFE photographer Alfred Eisenstaedt's favorite subject. No surprise, looking at his portrait of her (opposite), taken when she was 26. Moviegoers were enamored as well. The secret to her appeal? "Everything you see," the Italian actress told LIFE, "I owe to spaghetti."

JOHN R. HAMILTON

▲ HIS 165TH FILM, 1965'S *THE SONS OF KATIE ELDER,* WAS, SAID JOHN WAYNE, 57: "[A] RIDIN' JUMPIN' FIGHTIN' PICTURE."

PAUL SCHUTZER

▲ "THE BIGGEST U.S. RAGE SINCE ELIZABETH TAYLOR," SAID LIFE OF NATALIE WOOD, 23, IN 1962.

ALFRED EISENSTAEDT

SOPHIA LOREN, 1961

JOHN DOMINIS

Redford... Beatty... Fonda... Dunaway... Farrow

RALPH CRANE

CARLO BAVAGNOLI

▶ WITH WARREN BEATTY, 31, LIFE WROTE, "THERE IS NO WORRY OVER WHETHER SEDUCTION IS POSSIBLE, ONLY WHEN AND WHERE AND WHO'S NEXT" (1968).

▶ ▶ JANE FONDA, IN 1968's *BARBARELLA*

MILTON GREENE

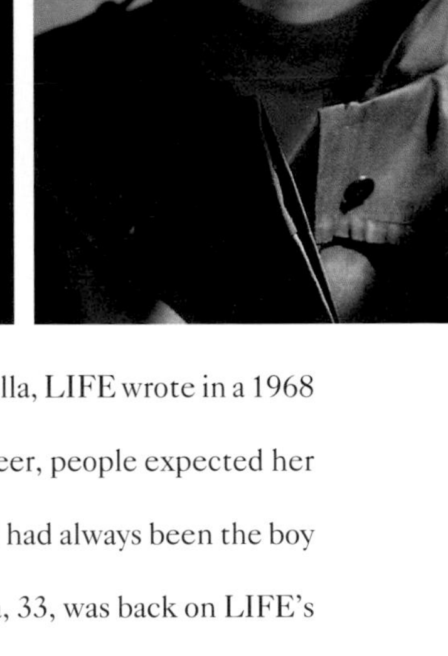

ALFRED EISENSTAEDT

▶ THROUGH HER ROLE IN *BONNIE AND CLYDE*, FAYE DUNAWAY, 26, "HAS DONE FOR THE BERET WHAT BARDOT DID FOR THE BIKINI" (1968).

▶ ▶ "I ONCE THOUGHT I'D LIKE TO HAVE 40 BABIES BY 40 OF THE MOST SUPER MEN IN THE WORLD," SAID MIA FARROW, 22, THEN MRS. FRANK SINATRA (1967).

◀ ROBERT REDFORD, 32, "STANDS A FAIR CHANCE OF BECOMING ONE OF THOSE RARE STARS WHO SUMS UP, ALL BY HIMSELF, THE SPIRIT OF HIS TIME—AS BRANDO DID FOR THE '50s" (1970).

About Jane Fonda's turn as vampy superheroine Barbarella, LIFE wrote in a 1968 cover story: "When Jane began her motion picture career, people expected her to become the girl next door just as her father [Henry] had always been the boy and man next door. Some girl next door." Three years later, Fonda, 33, was back on LIFE's cover, this time as a "busy rebel" speaking out for women's rights, unions and the Black Panthers. Said the actress, "I'm ready to support all struggles that are radical."

Ford . . . Winger . . . Turner . . . Streep

NANCY MORAN/SYGMA

THEO WESTENBERGER/GAMMA LIAISON

◀◀ HARRISON FORD, 39, WAS "ONE OF 1981's MOST MACHO MALES," LIFE DECLARED.

◀ AFTER HER BREAKOUT PERFORMANCE IN 1982's *AN OFFICER AND A GENTLEMAN,* DEBRA WINGER, 27, ADDRESSED HER REPUTATION. THE PRODUCERS, SHE SAID, "WERE PIGS. THEY WERE TERRIBLE. AND I WAS TERRIBLE BACK."

DOUGLAS KIRKLAND/SYGMA

◀ ABOUT THE CAMERA, KATHLEEN TURNER, 31, SAID IN 1985: "IT'S LIKE THIS ADORING DOG. IT JUST LOOKS AT YOU ALL THE TIME. IT'S SO FLATTERING, IT'S RIDICULOUS."

"No other actress her age can match her astounding range," said LIFE in a 1981 article titled "Marvelous Meryl." The magazine went on: "She is America's finest actress." A master of accents, Streep, 31, was perfecting a British one when she posed (right), dressed for her starring role in *The French Lieutenant's Woman.*

▶ MERYL STREEP, 1981

SNOWDON

E.J. CAMP/OUTLINE (2)

Washington . . . Costner . . . Foster . . . Pfeiffer . . . Hanks

▶ WITH 1989's *FIELD OF DREAMS*, KEVIN COSTNER, 34, WAS "THE YEAR'S HOMEBODY HEARTTHROB."

▶ ▶ JODIE FOSTER, 29, WORKED BOTH SIDES OF THE CAMERA IN 1991's *LITTLE MAN TATE*. "[HER] NEW CAREER," SAID LIFE, "COULD LEAD TO A SIGNAL ACHIEVEMENT—THE FIRST WOMAN TO WIN AN OSCAR FOR DIRECTING."

HELMUT NEWTON/SYGMA

HARRY BENSON

▶ MICHELLE PFEIFFER, WEARING THE HOPE DIAMOND, 1995

▶ ▶ LIFE WAS SURE TOM HANKS, 32, WOULD WIN AN OSCAR FOR 1988's *BIG*. BUT HANKS DIDN'T WIN HIS FIRST OSCAR UNTIL 1994, FOR *PHILADELPHIA*. THE NEXT YEAR HE WON HIS SECOND, FOR *FORREST GUMP*.

JOE MCNALLY

◀ IN 1989 THE MAGAZINE PICKED DENZEL WASHINGTON, 34, FROM A CROP OF NEW HOLLYWOOD FACES—AND PREDICTED STARDOM.

Of Michelle Pfeiffer (above), LIFE photographer Joe McNally observed: "She says more to the camera by lowering her eyelids than a fashion model can by jumping through hoops." McNally photographed the actress for an article about the Smithsonian's collection of priceless jewels. Said Pfeiffer, 37, about her two days of being swathed in diamonds and emeralds: "I could get used to this."

all. **IT WAS A SOLID AND EXHILARATING SURGE OF UP AND AWAY.”**

—ASTRONAUT JOHN GLENN, THE FIRST AMERICAN TO ORBIT THE EARTH, WRITING ABOUT HIS HISTORIC FLIGHT LIFE, MARCH 9, 1962

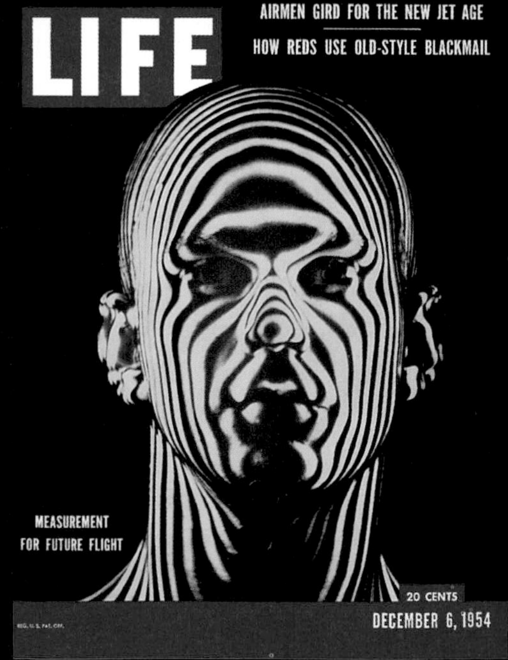

MAN IN THE JET AGE 12/6/54

60

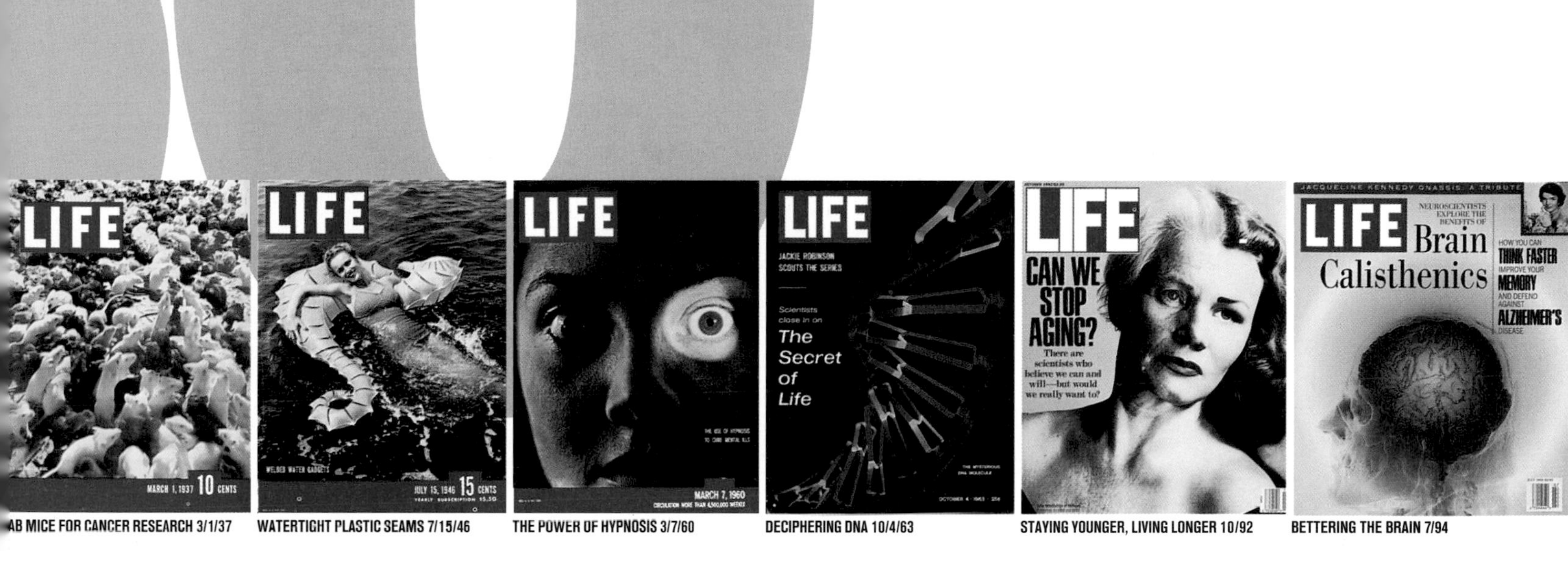

AB MICE FOR CANCER RESEARCH 3/1/37 WATERTIGHT PLASTIC SEAMS 7/15/46 THE POWER OF HYPNOSIS 3/7/60 DECIPHERING DNA 10/4/63 STAYING YOUNGER, LIVING LONGER 10/92 BETTERING THE BRAIN 7/94

overy

The questions are those often asked by children. Where did I come from? Why do people get sick? What's in outer space? In search of the answers, a photographer has captured on film the earliest stages of human development; doctors and scientists have identified the causes—and the cures—of many diseases; and astronauts have braved -300°F temperatures to repair a space telescope built so earthlings could see the sights of galaxies far, far away. But some of our discoveries have left us wondering whether we wouldn't be better off without them. How would our daily lives be different without the pervasive influence of television? Can genetic engineering be kept in check? What would the world be like if we had never entered the thermonuclear age?

Even the inventors of the atomic bomb could not fully imagine its devastating force.

MARIE HANSEN

▲ J. ROBERT OPPENHEIMER, 1945

▶ ATOMIC BOMB OVER NAGASAKI, JAPAN, AUGUST 9, 1945

NATIONAL ARCHIVES

"A single bomb of this type, carried by boat and exploded in a port, might very well destroy the whole port, together with some of the surrounding territory." That assessment by Albert Einstein arrived on President Franklin D. Roosevelt's desk in 1939. Six years later, on July 16, 1945, the first atomic bomb was detonated during a test in the desert near Alamogordo, N.Mex. On August 6, the U.S. dropped the weapon on Hiroshima, killing more than 70,000 and leveling the city. A second bomb, exploded over Nagasaki, killed some 40,000, forcing Japan's surrender and ending World War II. Lingering radiation in the two cities killed or maimed tens of thousands more. Having helped create this horrific tool of destruction, J. Robert Oppenheimer, the physicist who led the Manhattan Project, which developed the atomic bomb, opposed building an even more powerful hydrogen bomb. As did Einstein, who later lamented, "If only I had known, I should have become a watchmaker."

A novelty in one decade, a necessity the next, television isolated viewers while giving them a shared experience.

GEORGE SKADDING

▶ TV-WATCHING PARTY AT THE NUBERS, ERIE, PA., 1949

▲ PORTABLE TELEVISION, CHICAGO, 1948

More homes in the United States have one than have indoor plumbing. Next to sleeping, watching it is the activity to which Americans devote the most time—an average of seven hours a day. But in 1945, a Gallup poll found that only 19 percent of adults had ever actually seen this new thing called television. Though experimental TV broadcasts were being aired as early as the 1920s, it wasn't until after World War II that staring at "the box" really caught on. In the late 1940s, before there was an antenna on every roof, neighbors gathered to watch such programs as the quiz show *Cash and Carry,* the sitcom *The Goldbergs,* cooking tips on *I Love to Eat* and, every Tuesday night, the zany Uncle Miltie. For children of the baby boom, TV was both an electronic baby-sitter and a loyal friend—and the reason many know *The Mickey Mouse Club* theme song better than the words to the national anthem.

RALPH MORSE

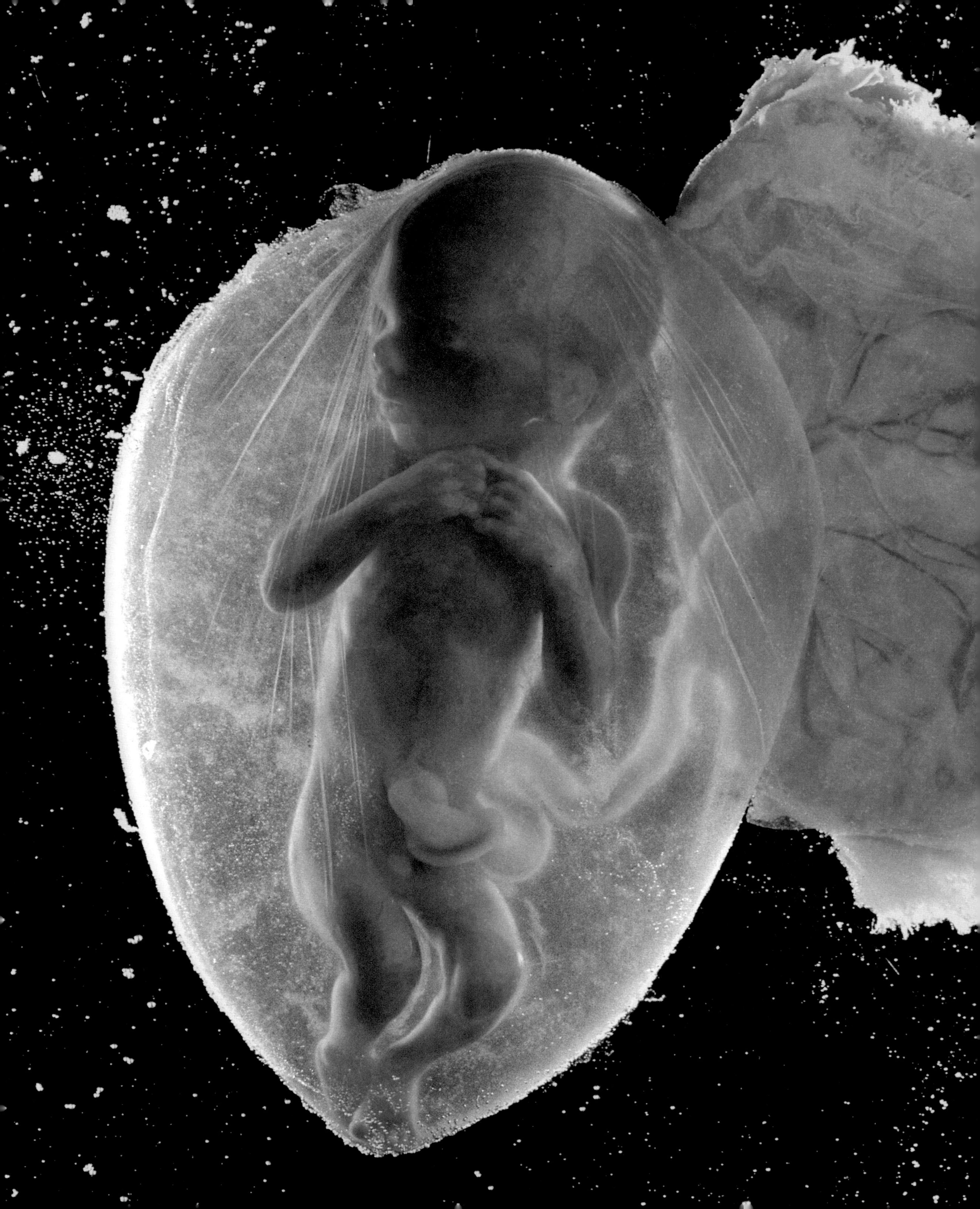

The first photo album of everybody's first trip: the journey before birth

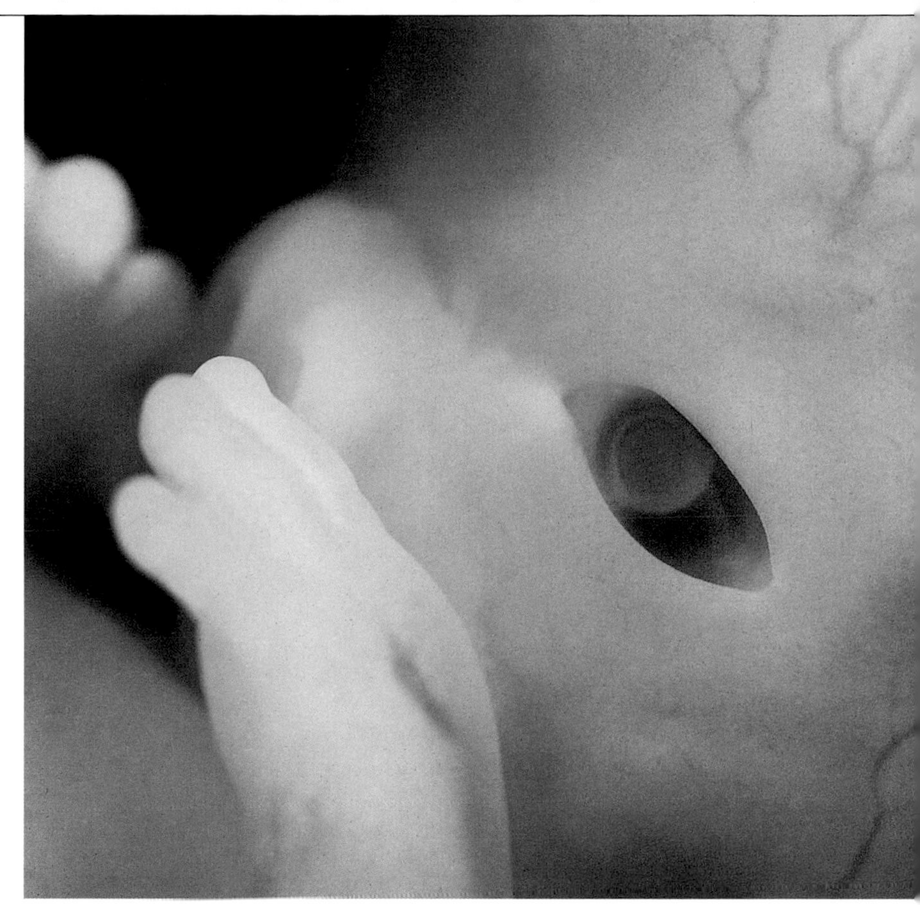

▲ EIGHT WEEKS GESTATION (APPROXIMATE SIZE FROM HEAD TO TOE: 1.5 INCHES)

We've all been there, but who remembers? In a groundbreaking article in the April 30, 1965, issue of LIFE, Swedish photographer Lennart Nilsson revealed what it looks like inside the womb. His photos were a scientific and aesthetic marvel. "This is like the first look at the dark side of the moon," said one gynecologist. In the years since, Nilsson's images of fetal development have been used by both sides in the rancorous debate over abortion. But the man who has actually witnessed a sperm enter an egg, and who has photographed every stage of human gestation, declares that even he cannot determine when life truly begins. "Maybe," he says, with a smile, "it starts with a kiss."

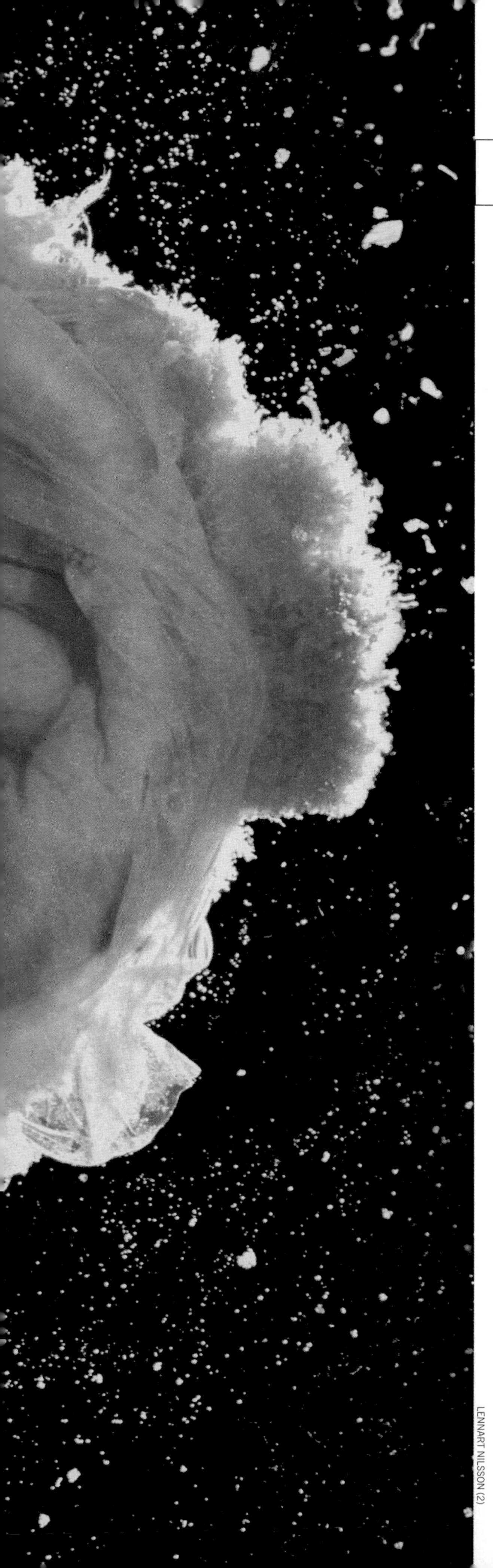

◀ 18 WEEKS GESTATION (APPROXIMATE SIZE: EIGHT INCHES)

LENNART NILSSON (2)

Jackie Gleason made "to the moon" a catchphrase. JFK made it a promise. *Apollo 11* made it a reality.

LYNN PELHAM

▲ ASTRONAUTS NEIL ARMSTRONG, MIKE COLLINS AND BUZZ ALDRIN, AFTER SPLASHDOWN, 1969

The Russians were winning. They sent up *Sputnik* (the first space satellite) in October 1957 and *Sputnik 2* (manned by Laika, the first space dog) a month later. In December, America's virgin attempt at satellite rocketry blew up on the launchpad. Upon John Glenn's orbit of the earth in 1962 (10 months behind the Russians), President Kennedy said: "We have a long way to go in this space race. But this is the new ocean, and I believe the U.S. must sail on it and be second to none." On July 20, 1969, America won the grand prize. At 10:56 p.m. EST, Neil Armstrong stepped onto the lunar landscape. He declared the moment a "giant leap for mankind." Back on earth, a note was placed on JFK's grave: "Mr. President, the *Eagle* has landed."

NASA

BUZZ ALDRIN, ARRANGING SEISMIC EQUIPMENT TO GAUGE LUNAR TREMORS, 1969

Amazing **medical advances** saved lives in the operating room—and created new ones in the lab.

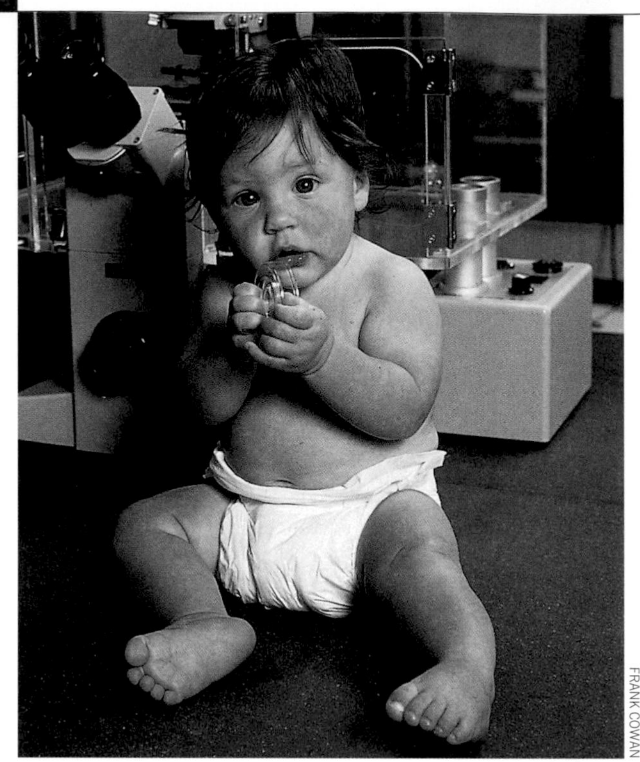

FRANK COWAN

▲ AMERICA'S FIRST "TEST-TUBE" BABY, ELIZABETH CARR, NINE MONTHS, VISITING THE EASTERN VIRGINIA MEDICAL SCHOOL LAB, WHERE SHE WAS CONCEIVED, 1982

Medical stories, fascinating to any curious mind, are often sources of hope. Having documented polio's tragedies, LIFE followed Jonas Salk's work on a vaccine, approved in 1955. Starting in the 1960s, the magazine reported on several failed attempts at organ transplants but by the early 1980s could show success. And when LIFE explained how infertile couples, desperate for a child, were able to conceive by in vitro fertilization, the magazine demystified what has since become a common, if often unsuccessful, procedure.

▶ LIVER TRANSPLANT SURGERY, ST. LUKE'S HOSPITAL, NEW YORK CITY, 1982

ERGUN CAGATAY

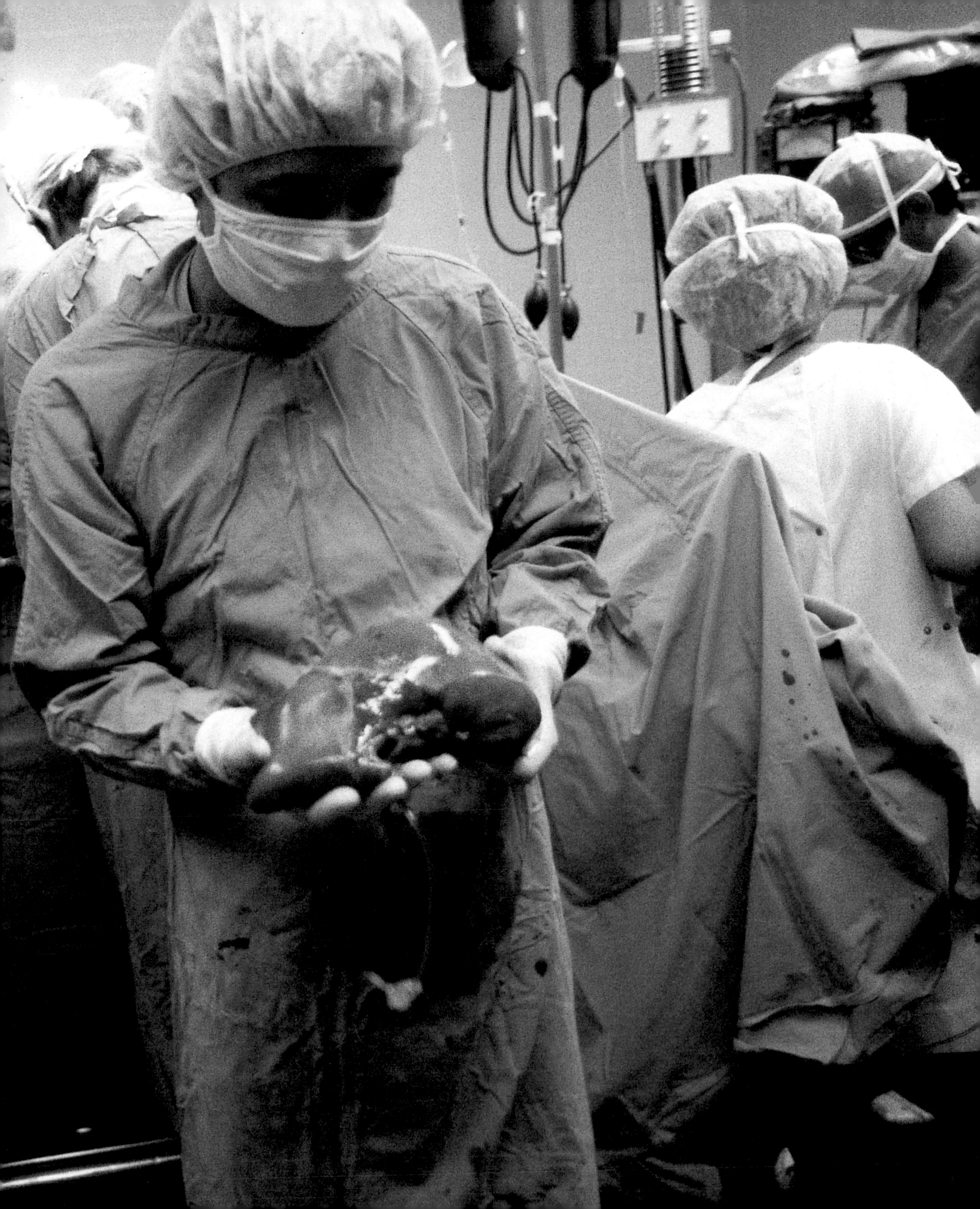

Peering deep into the universe, the **Hubble Space Telescope** searches for where it all began.

SPACE TELESCOPE SCIENCE INSTITUTE

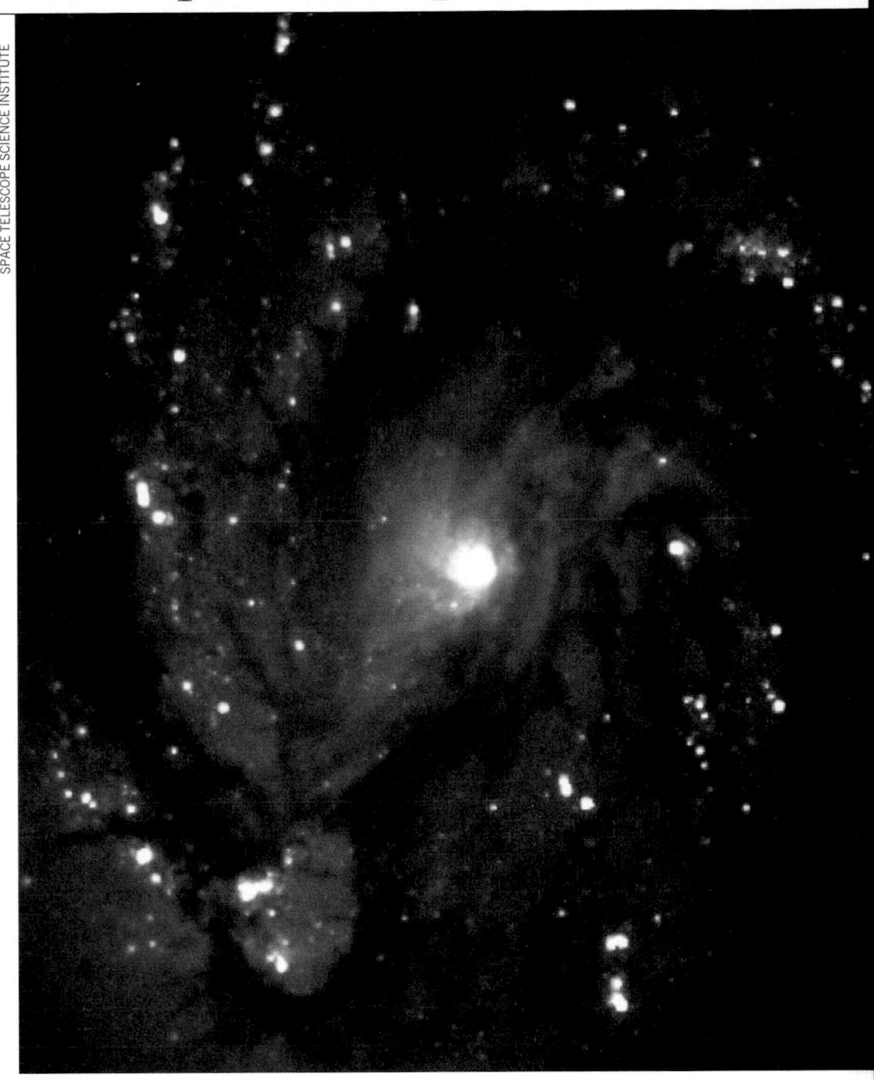

▲ **M100 GALAXY IN VIRGO CLUSTER, 1993**

Launched in April 1990, the Hubble Space Telescope was nearly a $1.6 billion fiasco: When it began sending photos back to earth two months later, scientists learned that the telescope was myopic. Optical adjustments made in 1993 by the crew of the space shuttle *Endeavour* ("We felt like the Maytag repairman," said astronaut Jim Crocker) fixed Hubble's vision—enabling it, and us, to see deeper into space than ever before. What was out there? Among other examples of intergalactic beauty: the light of objects that have been beaming at Earth for 10 billion years; evidence of a star that exploded in 1841; a view of a spiral galaxy, shaped like our own, located tens of millions of light-years away (above); and, from a place 400 million times more distant than the sun, six-trillion-mile-high columnar clouds of dust and hydrogen (the pinkish blobs at left) in the process of creating new stars. Astronomers hope a clear view of the universe's outer reaches will show them how galaxies are formed—and explain how the sun and the earth came to be.

◀ **EAGLE NEBULA, 1995**

JEFF HESTER & PAUL SCOWEN/ARIZONA STATE UNIVERSITY-NASA

Fashion, Fads

LIFE

THE SIREN LOOK FOR FALL

20 CENTS

SEPTEMBER 8, 1952

GLAMOROUS GOWNS 9/8/52

“Hug the hoop to the backside. Push hard with the right hand. Now rock, man, rock! Don’t twist. **SWING IT. SWAY IT.** You got it!”

—INSTRUCTIONS FOR THE SPIN-A-HOOP, AS QUOTED IN “WHOLE COUNTRY HOOPS IT UP IN A NEW CRAZE” LIFE, SEPTEMBER 8, 1958

"Teen-agers feel they cannot possibly afford to use last year's clothes, customs and language, so they set to work frantically, dreaming up outlandish fashions. Often the fads are momentary. Sometimes they catch on. But seldom," LIFE declared in 1947, "do they make much sense." (Case in point: phone-booth stuffing, all the rage in 1959.) But that doesn't mean the magazine hasn't paid serious attention to the frillier and sillier sides of life: Sixty years of pictures have captured the action of jitterbugs, bobby-soxers, streakers, disco dancers, muscle builders (including the pre-Hollywood Arnold Schwarzenegger, below, far right) and aerobicizers, to name just a few. When reporting on higher fashion, LIFE has tried to ensure that its stories make at least some sense to both the male and female halves of its readership. As one editor noted during the 1950s, a chignon became "a bun of hair at the nape of the neck" and "'smart' [was] a word to apply to a junior Phi Bete."

LOOK-ALIKE DOLLS 4/3/39

PEARLY FASHIONS 11/14/49

MOTORBOATING 6/1/59

MEN GO MOD 5/13/66

THE MINI VS. THE MIDI 3/13/70

SHAPING UP 10/82

In the midst of the Depression and a war, a cult of youth was born.

A word was added to the lexicon in the late 1930s: teenager. Finally distinct from children and grown-ups, America's adolescents discovered the pleasures of the slumber party, talking on the phone for hours, and the wearing of guys' clothing by girls (bottom right). The Congeroo (left), a hybrid of the Lindy Hop and the Conga, kept young dancers in shape. And in an effort to retain their own girlish figures, grown women turned to modern machines (top right) for a no-sweat workout. "As you look around the torture room and see the fat ladies," observed LIFE at one so-called slenderizing salon, "you're amazed at their complacent contentment. They are all getting thin without an effort." Later, when wartime shortages of nylon led women to paint on fake stockings (center), having fit legs—and not sweating—was essential.

THE CONGEROO, SAVOY BALLROOM, NEW YORK CITY, 1941

W. EUGENE SMITH

▶ FIGHTING FAT WITH THE SPLENDRO MASSAGER, 1940

ALFRED EISENSTAEDT

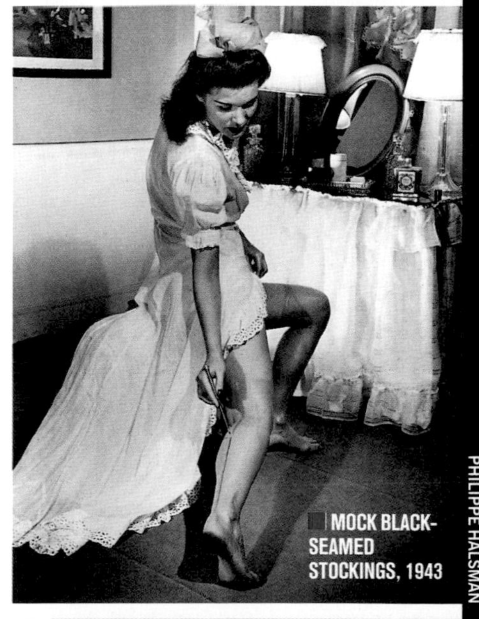

MOCK BLACK-SEAMED STOCKINGS, 1943

PHILIPPE HALSMAN

▶ RAG CURLS AND MEN'S PAJAMAS, 1944

NINA LEEN

Postwar affluence led to a serious **pursuit of leisure**—and silliness.

LOUIS FAURER

◀ **BINGO SKIRT FOR FOUR PLAYERS, 1953**

Americans had to stay on their toes to keep up with the latest fads. To junior high school girls in Evanston, Ill., in the fall of 1947, meeting friends before school to swap shoes (bottom left) was de rigueur. A more sophisticated fad, initiated by a New York designer, was the parlor-game skirt, or "conversation circle" (top left); it came with playing pieces in the pocket. And from Hollywood, which had cheered the nation through the Depression and World War II with escapist flicks, came ridiculous attempts at realism. "Natural Vision" required that audiences don 3-D glasses (opposite) to view such otherwise dull films as *Bwana Devil*, a movie about lions in Africa.

EDWARD CLARK

◀ **SHOE SWAPPING, 1947**

J. R. EYERMAN

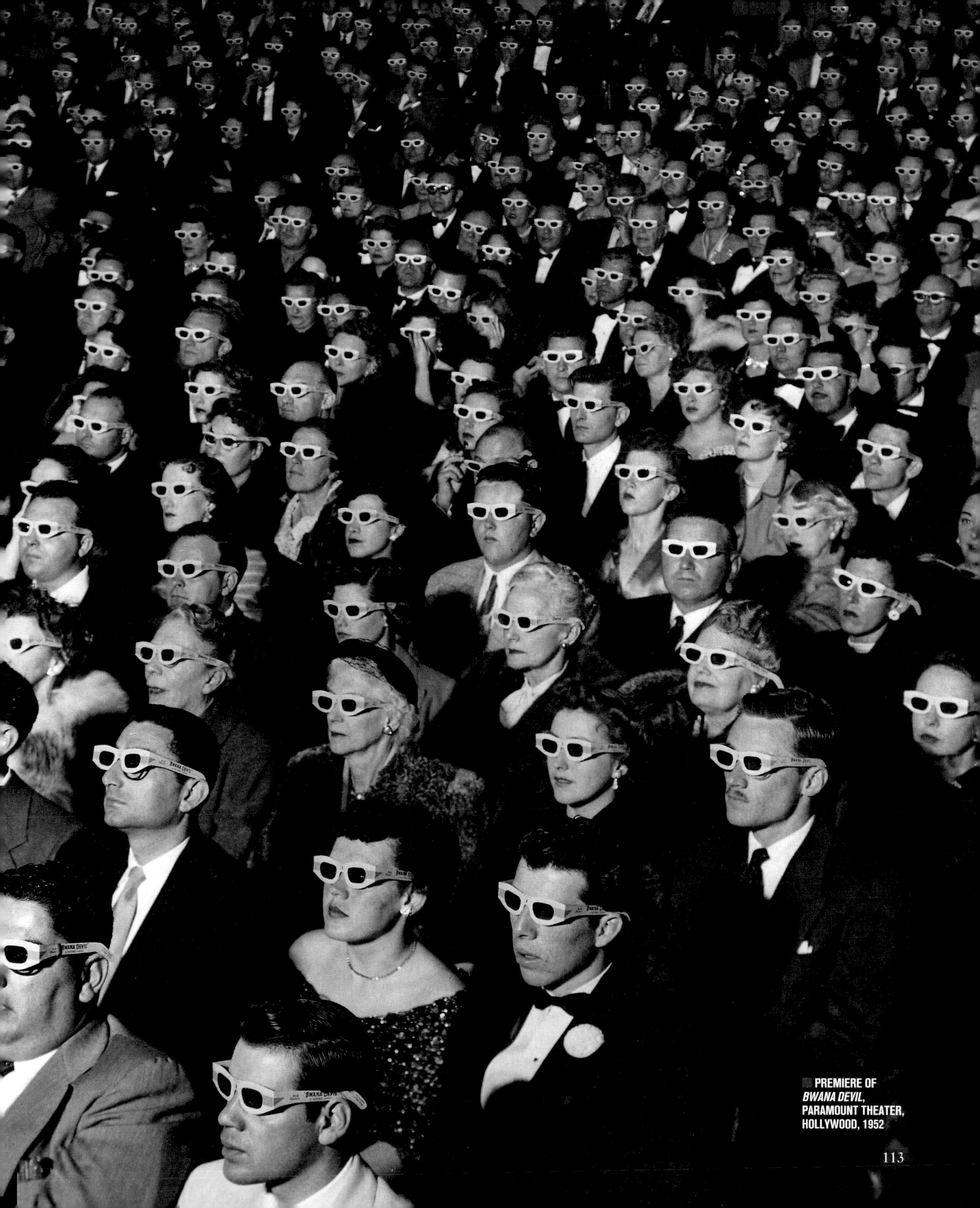

PREMIERE OF *BWANA DEVIL*, PARAMOUNT THEATER, HOLLYWOOD, 1952

Anything considered worth having was wanted by everyone, making many fads—like the hula hoop and the Jackie look—genuine **crazes**.

YALE JOEL

▲ **JACKIE WANNABES, NEW YORK CITY, 1961**

Its name had the exotic ring of the islands that would soon become America's 50th state. Although the action of the hula hoop (right) resembled the famed Hawaiian hula, the toy originated in Australia. A company named Wham-O imported the idea to the U.S. and by 1958 could hardly keep up with demand. Knockoffs helped fill the gap. The same was true in a way for a few genetically blessed (and pillbox-hatted) models when Jacqueline Kennedy moved into the White House. "Since the election my business has certainly picked up," Eugenia McLin (above, far right) told LIFE in 1961.

▶ **HULA-HOOPERS, DEERFIELD, ILL., 1958**

ARTHUR SHAY

Men's hair got long, women's skirts got short—and clothing sometimes disappeared altogether.

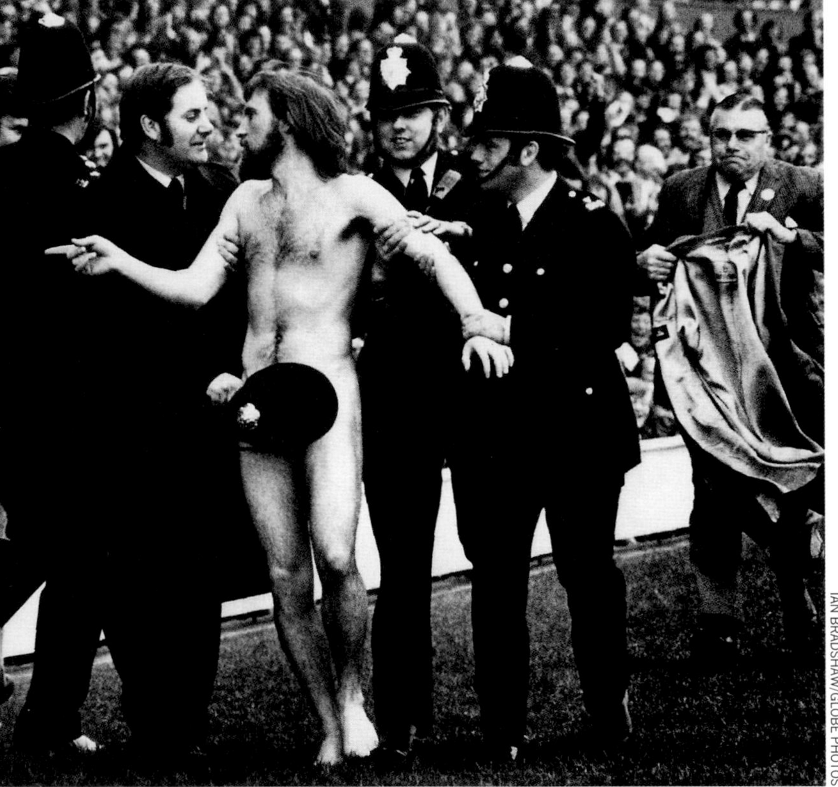

IAN BRADSHAW/GLOBE PHOTOS

◀ **RUGBY MATCH STREAKER, TWICKENHAM, ENGLAND, 1974**

Never trust anyone over 30. And don't dare be caught in something your mother or father would wear. Mini-dresses (right) designed for the under-21 set appeared in a LIFE story titled "Way-out Fashion in a Bizarre Young World." Further out, a guru of the Human Potential Movement, Paul Bindrim, called clothes "the modern mask" and encouraged his followers to shed them at encounter groups (bottom left). Streakers in the 1970s (top left) may have thought they were thoroughly modern, but they were actually quite retro: The trend of sprinting naked before a crowd dates back to the late 19th century.

◀ **ENCOUNTER GROUP, PALM SPRINGS, CALIF., 1968**

▶ **KNIT MINIDRESSES, 1967**

RALPH CRANE

BARRY KAPLAN

The **Hustle** came and went; not so the drive to tone flabby muscles.

ROXANNE LOWIT

▲ DISCO FEVER AT XENON, NEW YORK CITY, 1978

It is unlikely that the late 1970s and early '80s will be remembered for making a significant contribution to fashion. Tube tops, leisure suits and shiny synthetic fabrics—or shiny skin (above)—were the hot looks for those following the "shake, shake, shake your booty" drive of the disco beat. While the discotheque scene was sometimes linked to drug use (particularly cocaine), fitness was the muscle behind aerobics. Whether done in groups (right) or at home with a Jane Fonda exercise videotape, the mantra for all was "Feel the burn."

ENRICO FERORELLI

▶ AEROBICS CLASS AT THE SNOWBIRD SKI RESORT, LITTLE COTTONWOOD CANYON, UTAH, 1981

PAUL FUSCO / MAGNUM PHOTOS

Even clean-cut kids got grungy.

Gone were the days of little boys crying at the barbershop. Boys now *wanted* buzz cuts—so long as the coif featured a cartoon (like Bart Simpson), their initials (below) or another cool design. Such tidiness didn't necessarily last. Grunge, a style inspired by Seattle bands such as Pearl Jam and Nirvana, was widely embraced by teens and Gen X-ers (people in their early 20s), some of whom communed in a mosh pit at the very grungy Woodstock '94 music festival (left).

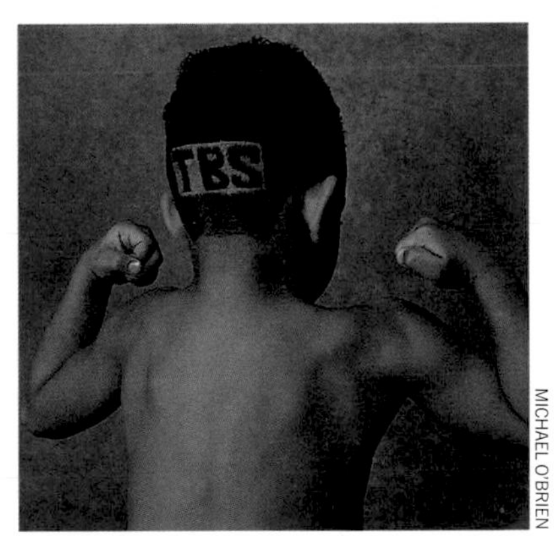

MICHAEL O'BRIEN

▲ **HAIR ART, 1990**

◀ **MUD-MOSHING, SAUGERTIES, N.Y., AUGUST 1994**

"For at least two minutes after the ship touched ground, **SURVIVORS CAME RUNNING OR STAGGERING THROUGH THE FLAMES**. Some escaped with slight injuries. Others were stark naked, their clothes and hair burned away, their skin hanging in shreds. Captain Ernst Lehmann, [who] stayed at his post until his clothes were ablaze, suffered such burns that he died the next day."

—FROM "THE *HINDENBURG* MAKES HER LAST LANDING AT LAKEHURST" LIFE, MAY 17, 1937

Dis

MOUNT KILAUEA 3/28/55

aster

HURRICANE CARLA 9/22/61

CRUISE SHIP ABLAZE 1/6/64

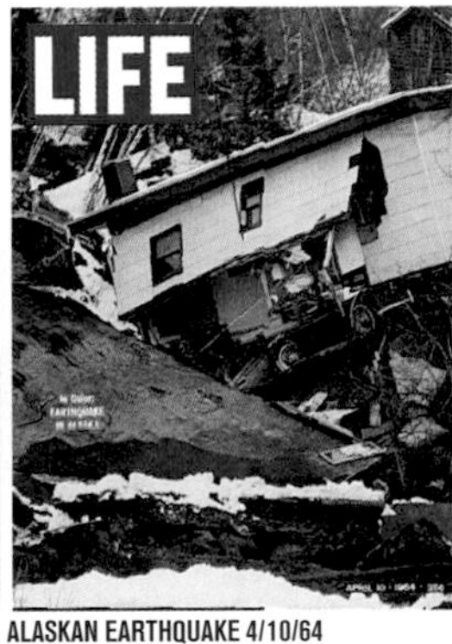

ALASKAN EARTHQUAKE 4/10/64

THREE MILE ISLAND, PENNSYLVANIA 5/79

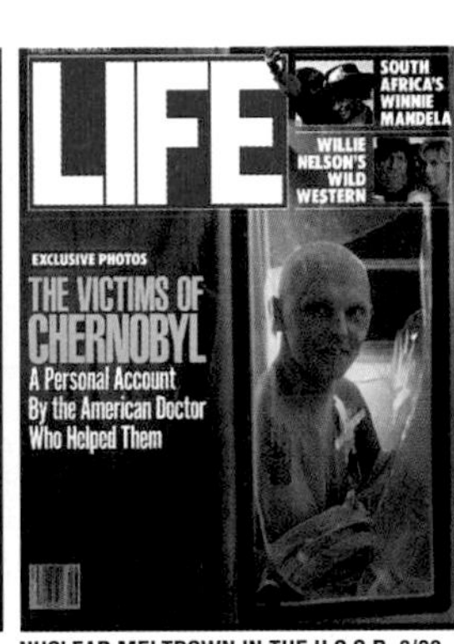

NUCLEAR MELTDOWN IN THE U.S.S.R. 8/86

PLANE CRASH IN IOWA 9/89

Among the earliest disasters reported in LIFE's pages was the explosion of the *Hindenburg*, the German zeppelin that burst into flames on May 6, 1937, while landing at an airstrip in Lakehurst, N.J. Yet it wasn't until Hawaii's Mount Kilauea erupted in 1955 that LIFE put a disaster story on the cover (left). Catastrophes—whether caused by nature's power or man's failure to troubleshoot his own inventions—make spectacular pictures. But what the camera captures is often unsettling, as is the randomness of the event itself and the possibility that tragedy will suddenly occur again. Will there be another accident at a nuclear power plant, like those at Three Mile Island and Chernobyl? Which flight will be the next to crash? Will tomorrow's earthquake—or hurricane or blizzard or volcanic eruption—be the Big One?

60

LUCILLE HANDBERG

Tornado

It destroys everything in its path, exploding buildings with a whirling funnel of air that spins at a velocity of more than 200 mph. When *The Wizard of Oz*, with its house-lifting twister, was released in 1939, the film was considered too frightening for children. In rural Minnesota, farm families had a look at the real thing when this tornado touched down, cutting a 50-foot-wide swath across the plains.

MINNESOTA, 1943

Earthquake

Nearly all of the city was destroyed in the war, but by the spring of 1948 more than half of Fukui (population 85,000) had been rebuilt. LIFE photographer Carl Mydans was on assignment to document the reconstruction when, at 5:14 p.m. on June 28, the earth cracked open. The tremors were so violent, said Mydans, that people "bounced about like popcorn." The 7.3-magnitude quake and resulting fires left more than 3,500 dead and the city in ruins again.

FUKUI, JAPAN, 1948

CARL MYDANS

LOOMIS DEAN

Tragedy at Sea

On July 25, the last night of the *Andrea Doria*'s voyage from Genoa to New York City, travelers in first class were dancing to "Arrivederci, Roma," while many in tourist watched a screening of *Foxfire*. One passenger later recalled glancing out a window at about 11:20 p.m. and seeing something that looked "like a city all lit up." Soon after, the *Stockholm,* an ocean liner whose bow had been built for cutting through ice, slammed into the *Doria*'s starboard side. Over the next six hours, lifeboats ferried 1,659 passengers and crew members to safety; 50 lives were lost. At 10:15 a.m. the *Andrea Doria* disappeared into the sea.

ATLANTIC OCEAN, 45 MILES SOUTH OF NANTUCKET, MASS., 1956

Flood

It was not a flood of biblical proportions. But the torrential rains and 90-mph winds that swept through central and northern Italy were especially brutal to Florence. Buildings and streets collapsed, ancient manuscripts were turned to pulp, precious works of art—by Giotto, Ghirlandaio, Botticelli—were soaked by water, oil and mud. From the safety of his pedestal in the Accademia, Michelangelo's *David* was a witness to the destruction.

FLORENCE, ITALY, 1966

DAVID LEES

Famine

Devastating famine plagued a widespread area of Africa—including Niger, Chad, Ethiopia and the Sudan—beginning in the early 1980s. The immediate cause was drought. The underlying causes: rapid population growth, mismanaged agricultural programs and, most cruelly, civil wars. In Mali, starving women and children walked across the completely dried-up Lake Ságuibin in search of relief.

GOUNDAM, MALI, 1985

SEBASTIAO SALGADO/MAGNUM PHOTOS

Terror in the sky

Aloha Airlines Flight 243 could be considered an argument for either collective prayer or the faithful use of seat belts. The 737's fuselage ripped apart at 24,000 feet—possibly due to corrosion, said inspectors—during a short trip from Hilo to Honolulu. Passengers sang hymns as the pilot steered the torn craft to safety. Of the 95 people on board, one, a flight attendant standing in the aisle, was killed. She had been sucked out of the jet when the plane blew open.

KAHULUI AIRPORT, MAUI, 1988

ROBERT NICHOLS/BLACK STAR

“This used to be DiMaggio's. I had the locker next door. It was my first year and **I WAS TOO SCARED TO TALK TO HIM.** So I used to peek around the corner and just stare at him when I knew he wasn't looking.”

—MICKEY MANTLE, REMINISCING ABOUT HIS ROOKIE YEAR

LIFE, JULY 30, 1965

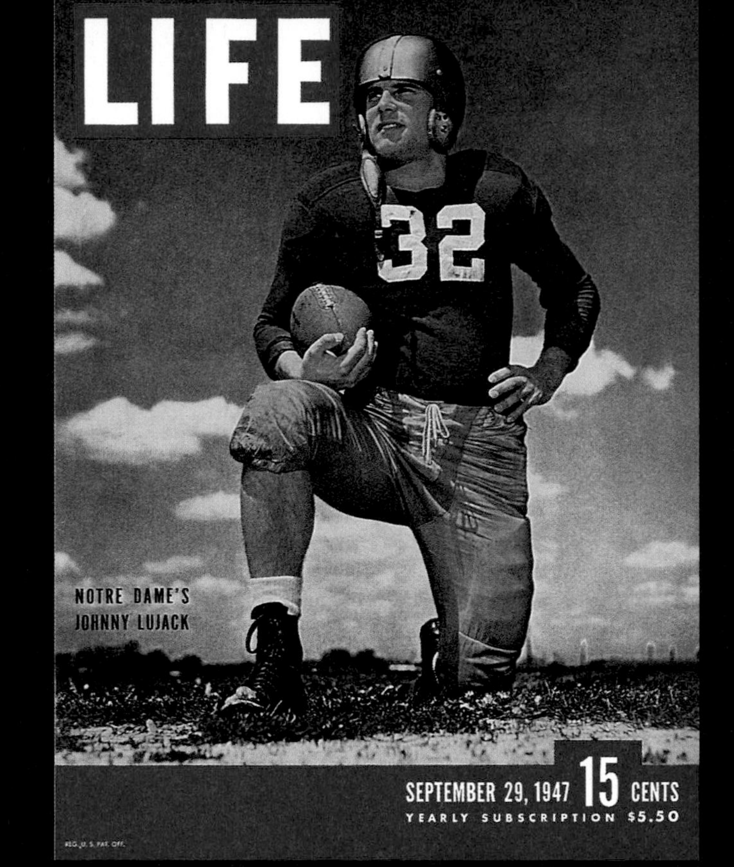

ALL-AMERICAN QUARTERBACK 9/29/47

One of the first sports stories to appear in LIFE was an article about two on-ice brawls involving the New York Rangers. "Nothing livens up a professional hockey game," noted the magazine in January 1937, "like a couple of good fistfights." (Some things never change.) The first professional athlete to appear on LIFE's cover was Brooklyn Dodger Tom Winsett, in April 1938, who batted a dismal .237 the previous season. More often, however, for 60 seasons—and 26 Olympics—LIFE has been witness to athletic excellence: the greatness of Jackie Robinson, who broke baseball's color barrier; the intensity of five-time middleweight champ Sugar Ray Robinson; the classic home-run race between teammates Mickey Mantle and Roger Maris; the grace of figure skater Peggy Fleming; the drive of speed skater Bonnie Blair, and the prowess of so many incredible others.

60

JACKIE ROBINSON 5/8/50

SUGAR RAY ROBINSON 4/7/58

MICKEY MANTLE & ROGER MARIS 8/18/61

PEGGY FLEMING STRIKES GOLD 2/23/68

SPEED SKATER BONNIE BLAIR 2/88

SPRINTER GWEN TORRENCE 7/96

letes

IN 1945, GJON MILI ATTACHED TINY LIGHTS TO THE BOOTS OF FIGURE SKATER CAROL LYNNE TO PHOTOGRAPH THE PATTERNS OF HER SPINS AND LEAPS, INCLUDING THE "FAWN JUMP" PICTURED HERE.

Carol Lynne and Alice Marble leapt for the camera; Patty Berg and "Yankee Clipper" Joe DiMaggio made winning swings.

GJON MILI (2)

AP

W. EUGENE SMITH

JOE DiMAGGIO, 1941

▲ PATTY BERG, 20, WINNER OF THE WOMEN'S NATIONAL GOLF CHAMPIONSHIP, 1938

▲▲ IN 1939, LIFE SAID OF ALICE MARBLE, 25, THE TOP-RANKED WOMAN IN U.S. TENNIS, "IF SHE HAD HER WAY, SHE WOULD PLAY ONLY IN MEN'S TOURNAMENTS." ALSO NOTED: "SHE IS A PRETTY GIRL WHO LOOKS WELL IN SHORTS."

What baseball experts value most highly in a player is a mysterious quality called baseball instinct," LIFE wrote in 1939. "In this respect, Joe DiMaggio is without a peer." Two years later, on July 1, 1941, LIFE photographer W. Eugene Smith found the 26-year-old centerfielder (above, right) lazing on a steamer trunk outside the Yankee clubhouse. Moments later, in his first at bat in the second half of a doubleheader against the Boston Red Sox, DiMaggio tied the major-league record for consecutive games with a hit—44. He would go on to hit safely in 56 straight games, a feat that remains unmatched more than a half century later.

Andrea Mead schussed in Sun Valley; Dodger wannabes squatted in the Florida sun.

▲ ANDREA MEAD, 15, PREPARING FOR THE 1948 WINTER OLYMPICS IN SUN VALLEY, IDAHO. FOUR YEARS LATER SHE WOULD WIN TWO GOLD MEDALS IN OSLO.

In the spring of 1948, more than 500 aspiring major-league baseball players were invited to "Dodgertown," the Brooklyn Dodgers rookie training camp. Housed for eight weeks at an abandoned wartime naval air station in Vero Beach, Fla., the hopefuls had to bounce out of bed at 6:45 a.m., attend strategy sessions and participate in mass calisthenics (right). Many would get a chance to play with one of the Dodgers' 25 minor-league teams. The rest, reported LIFE, would be "taken aside and quietly advised" to find other work.

BROOKLYN DODGERS ROOKIE SPRING TRAINING, 1948

GEORGE SILK (2)

CASSIUS CLAY AFTER KNOCKING OUT CHARLEY POWELL, PITTSBURGH, JANUARY 24, 1963

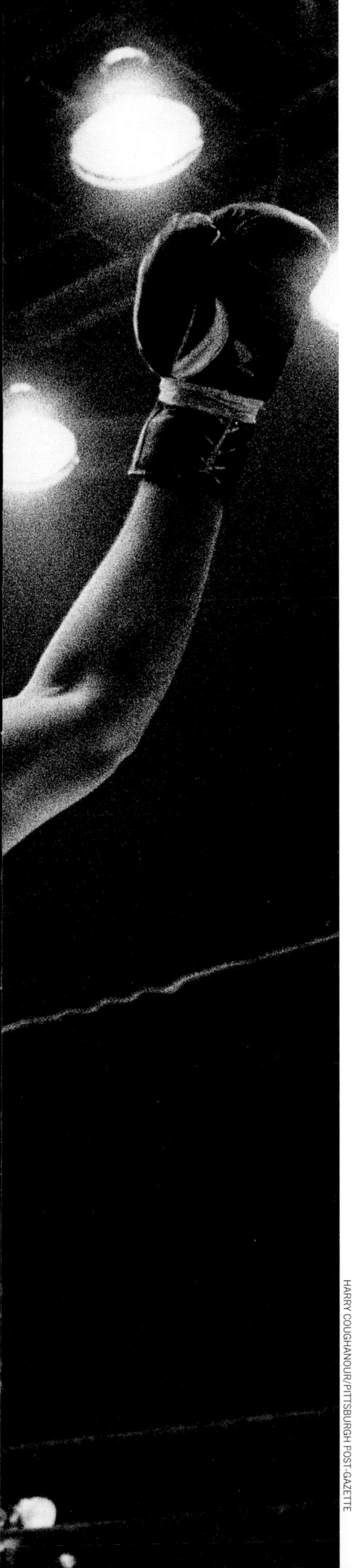

Cassius Clay boasted, Arthur Ashe smashed, and Y.A. Tittle knelt dazed in the end zone.

"Cassius Clay has the loudest—and most lyrical—mouth in the history of boxing and the fists to back it up," wrote LIFE in 1963. Accompanying the article was a poem the 21-year-old Louisville prize-fighter (left) composed himself. The title: ". . . I'm the greatest." (A stanza: "What a frustrating feeling I'm sure it must be / To be hit by blows you can't even see.") Clay could, as he liked to say, "float like a butterfly, sting like a bee," and his lightning-quick jabs were the undoing of Sonny Liston, whom he defeated in February 1964 for the heavyweight title. Soon after, Clay took the Muslim name Muhammad Ali.

▼ NEW YORK GIANTS QUARTERBACK Y.A. TITTLE, AFTER BEING SACKED BY A PITTSBURGH STEELER IN 1964, THE LAST SEASON OF HIS 17-YEAR CAREER

▶ ARTHUR ASHE IN 1965, TWO YEARS AFTER HE BECAME THE FIRST BLACK PLAYER ON A U.S. DAVIS CUP TEAM. IN 1968 HE WOULD WIN THE U.S. OPEN.

BOB GOMEL

HARRY COUGHANOUR/PITTSBURGH POST-GAZETTE

MORRIS BERMAN/PITTSBURGH POST-GAZETTE

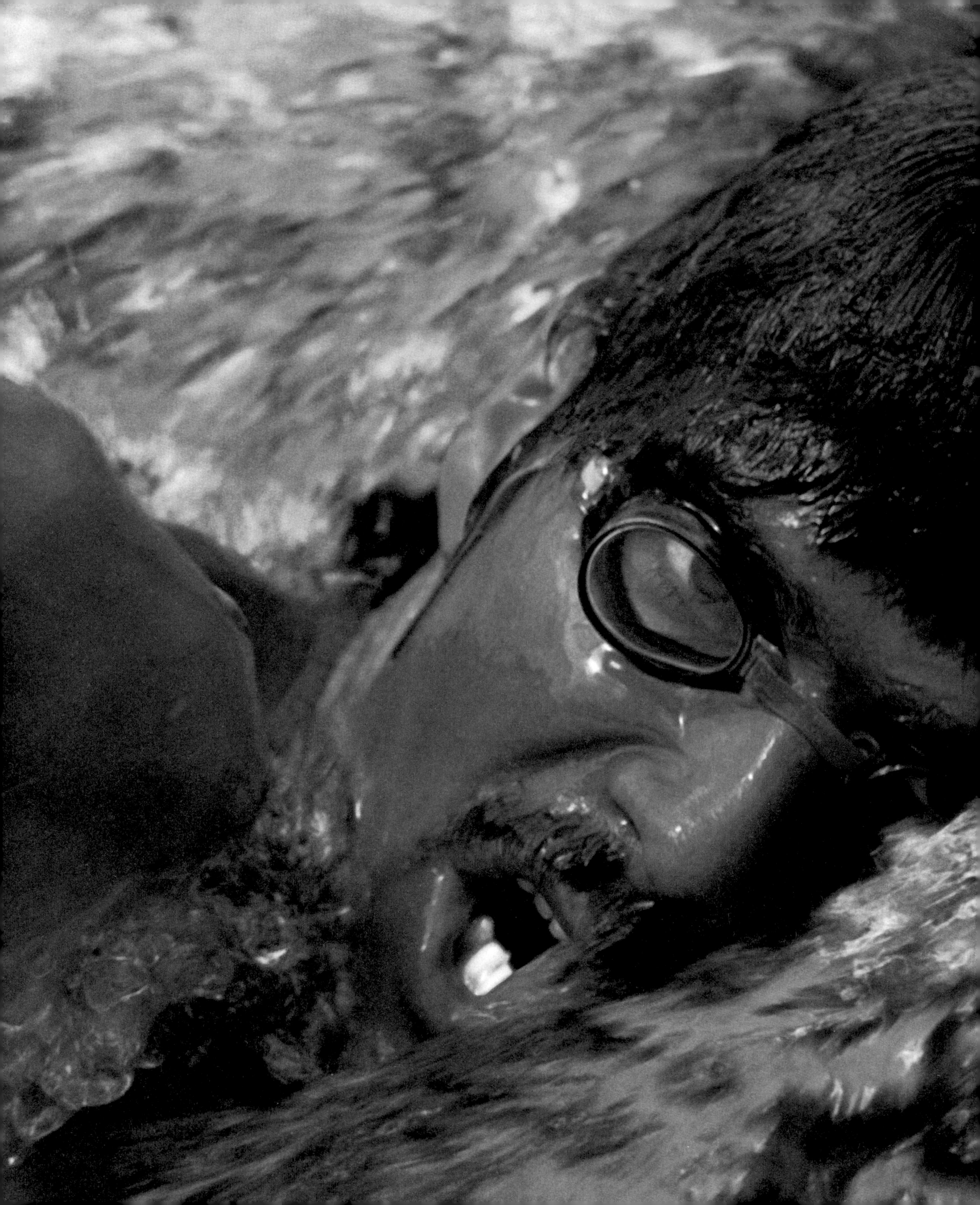

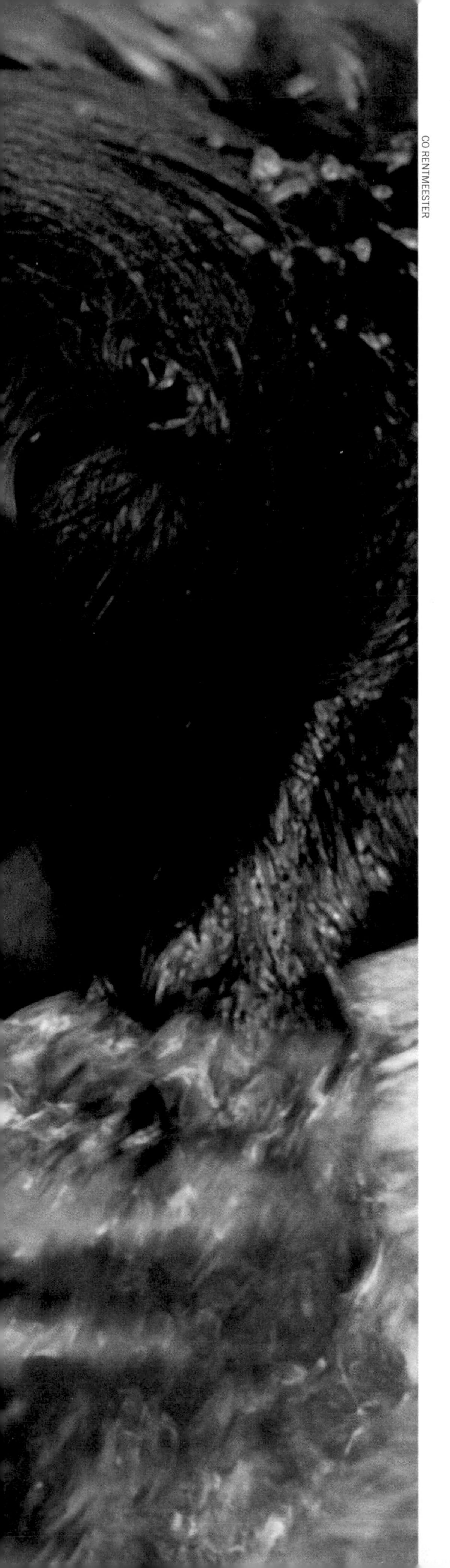

CO RENTMEESTER

Joe Namath swaggered, Mark Spitz swam, but Cathy Rigby slipped.

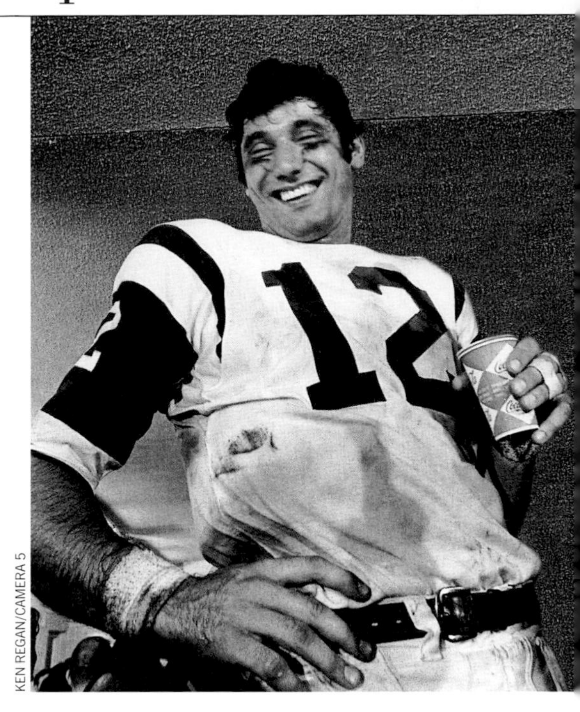

KEN REGAN/CAMERA 5

▶ JOE NAMATH, 25, TOASTS HIS SUPER BOWL WIN, 1969.

When rookie Joe Namath received an unheard-of $400,000 three-year deal to join the New York Jets in 1965, it sent a shock wave through professional football. But the investment paid off in 1969 when the charismatic quarterback led his AFL team to victory against the NFL's Baltimore Colts in Super Bowl III. Not only did money alter the playing field of athletics in the late 1960s and early 1970s, so did politics. In Munich in 1972, the murders of 11 members of Israel's Olympic team by Arab terrorists cast a long shadow over the Games. And it tarnished the luster of the unprecedented seven gold medals won by American swimmer Mark Spitz (left).

◀ MARK SPITZ, 22, TRAINING FOR THE 1972 OLYMPICS

▼ IN 1972, CATHY RIGBY, 19, FAILED TO WIN AN OLYMPIC MEDAL AT MUNICH, DESPITE BEING BILLED AS "ONE OF THE TWO BEST WOMEN GYMNASTS IN THE WORLD." THE OTHER, THE U.S.S.R.'S LUDMILA TOURISCHEVA, WON A GOLD.

JOHN DOMINIS

Michael Jordan soared, Kurt Thomas spun, and Carl Lewis sprinted for gold.

CO RENTMEESTER

◀ CARL LEWIS, 23, AFTER WINNING HIS FOURTH GOLD MEDAL AT THE 1984 OLYMPICS IN LOS ANGELES

▲ IN 1984, MICHAEL JORDAN, 21, WAS A COLLEGE JUNIOR, AND MEMBER OF THE U.S. OLYMPIC TEAM.

In the Olympics, only figure skaters and synchronized swimmers get separate marks for artistic merit. But in the pages of LIFE the artistry of many of the world's greatest athletes has been preserved forever: the victorious leap of track-and-field star Carl Lewis; the aerial wizardry of gymnast Kurt Thomas; the gravity-defying hang time of basketball phenom Michael Jordan, whose classic leap (above) would later be stitched into a logo on his own line of Nike athletic gear.

IN 1979, KURT THOMAS, 22, TOLD LIFE HE HOPED A GOLD MEDAL IN MOSCOW WOULD MAKE HIM "THE BEST IN THE WORLD." HIS DREAMS WERE DASHED WHEN THE U.S. BOYCOTTED THE 1980 OLYMPICS BECAUSE OF THE SOVIET INVASION OF AFGHANISTAN.

JOHN G. ZIMMERMAN (2)

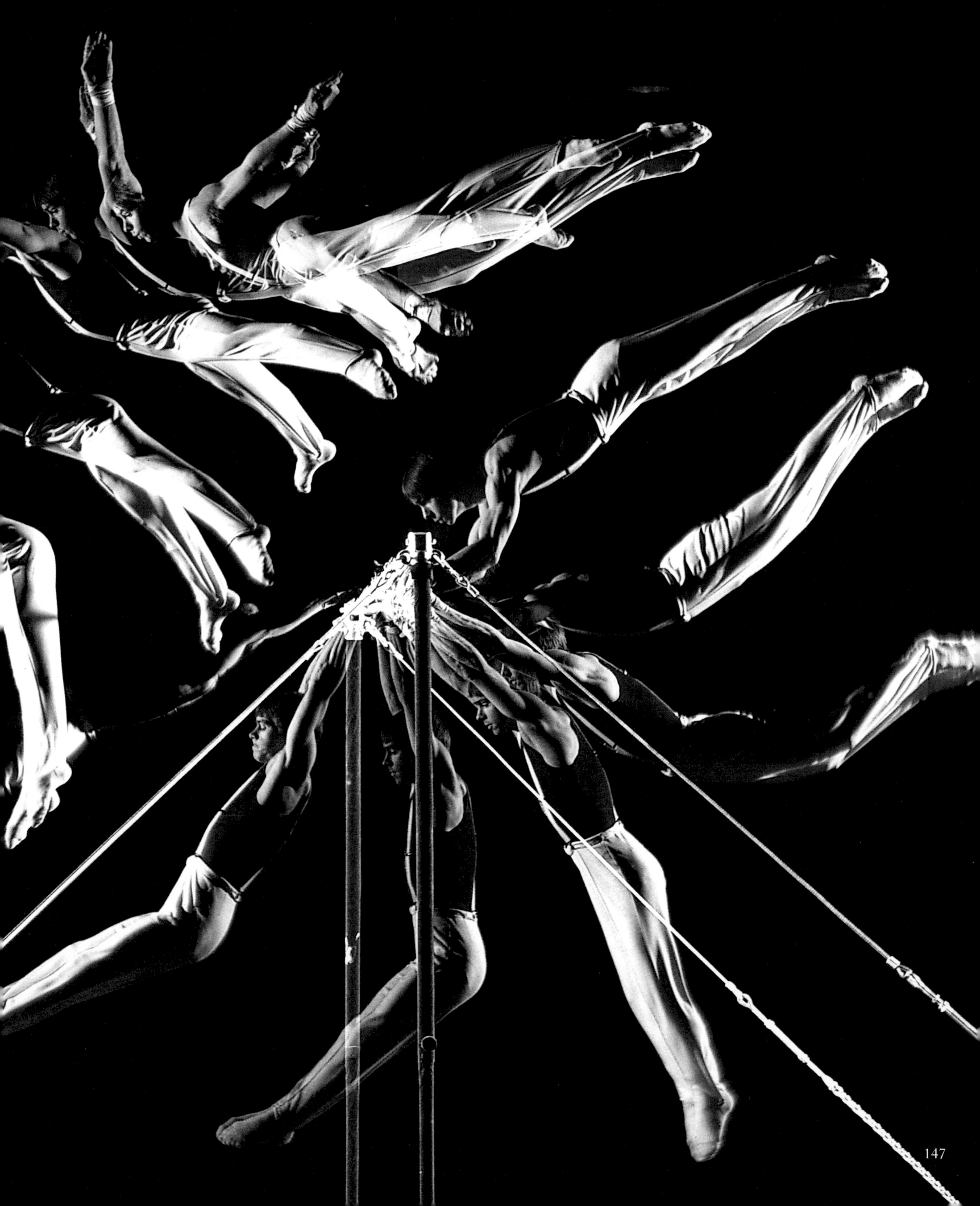

Oksana Baiul floated on ice, **Dennis Rodman** showed his sweet side, and the U.S. water polo team bared all.

CO RENTMEESTER

◀ OKSANA BAIUL, 16, AN ORPHAN FROM THE UKRAINE, WAS "THE SWAN OF ODESSA," SAID LIFE AFTER SHE WON GOLD AT LILLEHAMMER IN 1994.

▶ DENNIS RODMAN AND MOM, 1996

JOE MCNALLY

◀ IN 1996, LIFE CELEBRATED THE OLYMPIC BODY BY SNEAKING A PEEK AT THE PERFECT BODIES OF U.S. WATER POLO TEAM MEMBERS (FROM LEFT) RICK McNAIR, ALEX ROUSSEAU, CHRIS HUMBERT AND CHRIS DUPANTY.

Even the biggest and baddest of athletes occasionally needs his mommy, as LIFE discovered when it saw Chicago Bulls forward Dennis Rodman, 34, cuddle up with his mom, Shirley (right). Modesty and humility are qualities not always associated with extravagantly paid superstar athletes. But, said the mother of one of the premier rebounders in the NBA: "The Dennis you meet and the Dennis you see on the court are two different things. It's like with movie stars: You put on a performance, and then the performance is over."

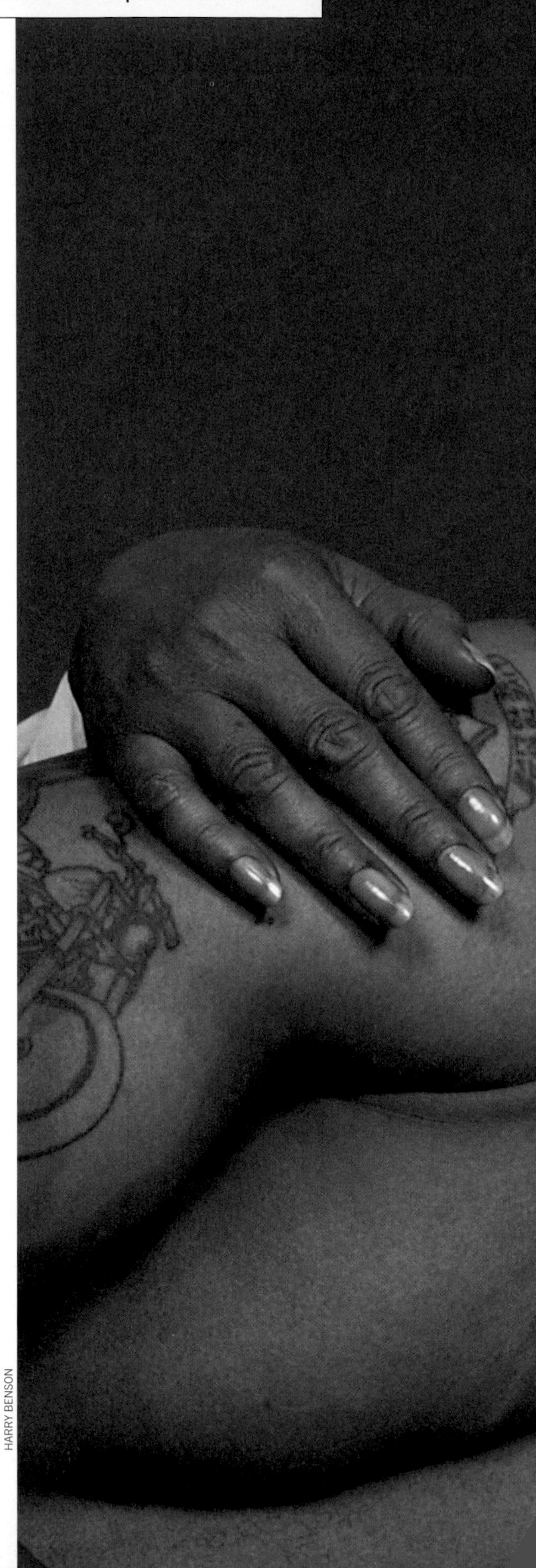

HARRY BENSON

Protest

“He often said an unearned suffering is redemptive, and **IF YOU GIVE YOUR LIFE TO A CAUSE** in which you believe and which is right and just—and it is—and if your life comes to an end as a result of this, then your life could not have been lived in a more redemptive way. And I think that this is what my husband has done. But then I ask the question: How many men must die before we can really have a free and true and peaceful society? How long will it take?”

—CORETTA SCOTT KING, SPEAKING AT A CIVIL RIGHTS RALLY IN MEMPHIS THE DAY BEFORE MARTIN LUTHER KING JR.'S FUNERAL LIFE, APRIL 19, 1968

STUDENT REBELLION AT HARVARD 4/25/69

& Unrest

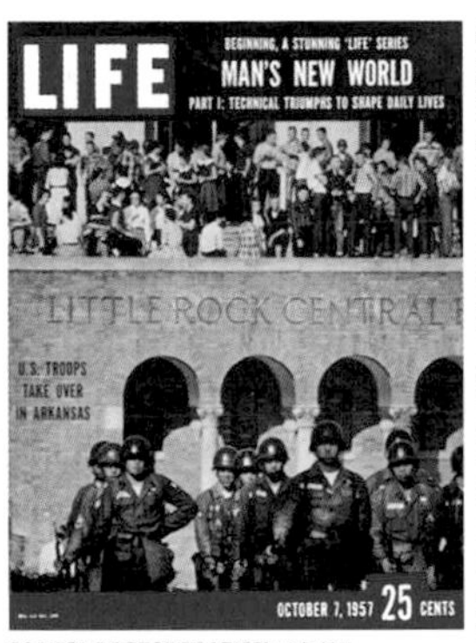

SCHOOL DESEGREGATION 10/7/57

AVOIDING THE DRAFT 12/9/66

RIOTS IN NEWARK 7/28/67

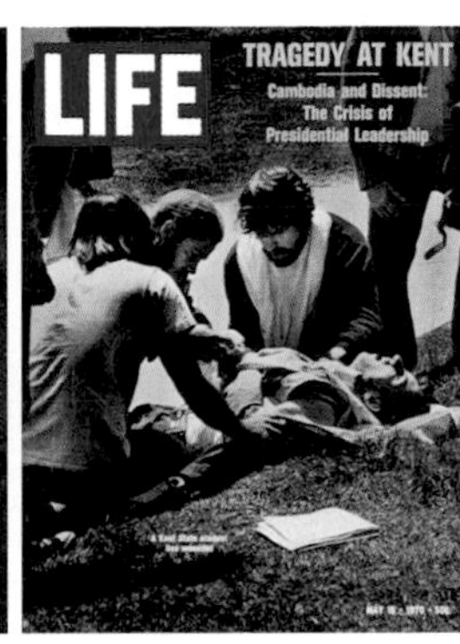

KENT STATE KILLINGS 5/15/70

ALL ABOUT WOMEN'S LIB 8/13/71

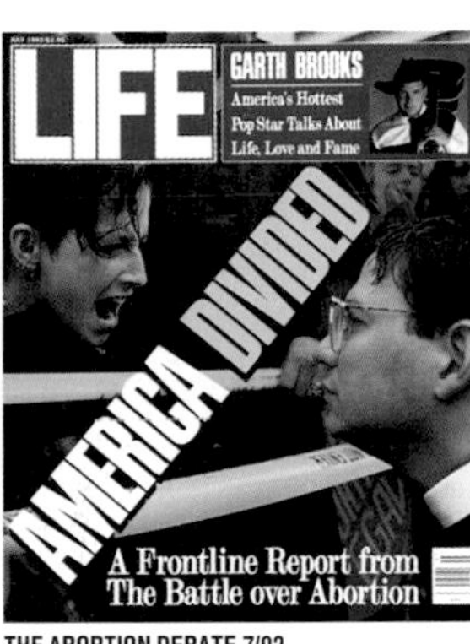

THE ABORTION DEBATE 7/92

Feet often speak louder than words. Not merely the thunder of them, but the sight of vast numbers of people marching with a unified purpose. During the past 60 years protesters have hit the pavement for women's rights, workers' rights and civil rights. They have paraded against war and for democracy. They have held walk-outs, sit-downs, sit-ins, be-ins, love-ins and, to demand government action on the AIDS epidemic, die-ins. Many men and women have lost their lives fighting for their beliefs: Civil rights leaders knew their activism could be fatal; antiwar demonstrators at Kent State did not. But sometimes it is the activists who cause the harm. Think of the McCarthy witch-hunts, the Middle East hostage crises, the riots in our streets.

60

WILLIAM VANDIVERT

▲ RALLY IN CADILLAC SQUARE, DETROIT, MARCH 23, 1937

▶ REPUBLIC STEEL STRIKE, CHICAGO, MAY 30, 1937

In April 1937, LIFE reported that sit-down strikes in the U.S. had "reached epidemic proportions." The new labor union tactic, used earlier that year against General Motors and Chrysler, was successful largely because employees stopped working and remained camped out at the factories to prevent replacement hires. Some labor protests—including a traffic-stopping rally of 60,000 (above), organized as a show of union might and support for sit-down strikers—were staged without serious incident. But at many others (right), both strikers and police turned violent.

ASSOCIATED PRESS

Fed up with the abuses of industry, **labor unions** urged workers to sit down in order to stand up for their rights.

Panic about the red menace made America ripe for McCarthyism.

MARTHA HOLMES

▲ ACTORS DANNY KAYE, JUNE HAVOC, HUMPHREY BOGART (STANDING) AND LAUREN BACALL (SEATED), HOUSE COMMITTEE ON UN-AMERICAN ACTIVITIES HEARINGS, WASHINGTON, D.C., OCTOBER 1947

The Soviet Union, once an ally, was now an enemy. Eastern Europe was being engulfed by the communists. Was America next? That fear was the force behind the House Committee on Un-American Activities, which set out to uncover spies and communist sympathizers in the U.S., most notably in Hollywood. In 1947, Humphrey Bogart and wife Lauren Bacall (above) joined fellow actors in support of screenwriters, producers and others subpoenaed by the committee. Those who refused to cooperate were blacklisted, their careers often ruined. Joseph McCarthy, the junior senator from Wisconsin, further fueled the hysteria during a 1950 GOP gathering in Wheeling, W.Va., when he waved what he claimed was a list of 205 communist spies who had infiltrated the State Department. He produced no evidence for his charges, but his crusade flourished. McCarthy peaked—then plummeted—in 1954, when he pursued alleged communists in the Army and was censured by the Senate.

HANK WALKER

SEN. JOSEPH McCARTHY, WITH AIDE ROY COHN, ARMY-McCARTHY HEARINGS, WASHINGTON, D.C., APRIL 1954

REV. MARTIN LUTHER KING JR., BEING BOOKED BY THE MONTGOMERY, ALA., POLICE, SEPTEMBER 1958

CHARLES MOORE/BLACK STAR

The nation's soul was tested in the long, acrimonious and often bloody struggle for civil rights.

In 1954 the Supreme Court issued a unanimous ruling in *Brown* v. *Board of Education of Topeka*: Separate but equal, the justices declared, was *not* equal. In a related opinion the following year, the Court ordered that the nation's schools be integrated with "all deliberate speed." But desegregation—in the classroom and in daily life—would be long in coming. In December 1955 seamstress Rosa Parks was arrested on a Montgomery, Ala., bus for refusing to give her seat to a white man. Outraged, local minister Rev. Martin Luther King Jr. led the city's blacks in a successful yearlong bus boycott. By 1963, when King gave his I Have a Dream speech in Washington, D.C., he was the recognized leader of the civil rights movement. "There will be neither rest nor tranquillity in America until the Negro is granted his citizenship rights," King said. Progress came with the 1964 Civil Rights Act. But four years later, King, 39, a man who preached nonviolence, was cut down on a Memphis motel balcony by an assassin's bullet.

Vying for political attention, two movements called for an

end to war: one in Vietnam, the other between the sexes.

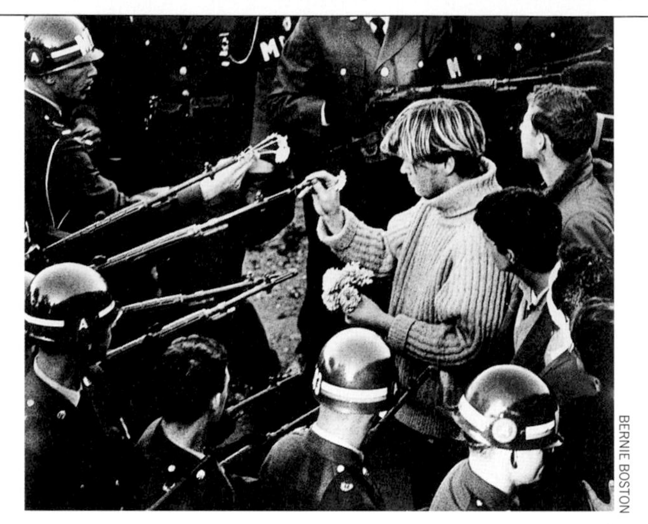

BERNIE BOSTON

▲ ANTIWAR PROTEST AT THE PENTAGON, OCTOBER 21, 1967

When men are dying overseas, domestic issues—especially those important to women—tend to end up on the back burner. Suffrage for American women had to wait until after the First World War. And it was the stifling domesticity of post–World War II America that gave rise to the frustrations Betty Friedan, a New York housewife, voiced in her best-selling manifesto *The Feminine Mystique.* Published in 1963, the book ignited the modern women's movement. But as U.S. involvement in Vietnam escalated, women's quest for equality was again overshadowed. Antiwar protests, including draft-card burnings and marches on Washington (above), fast became the passion of many of the nation's young. As LIFE noted in 1970, "Generally speaking, women do not have the choices and opportunities in lifestyle that are available to men."

JOHN OLSON

■ WOMEN'S RIGHTS MARCH ON FIFTH AVENUE, NEW YORK CITY, AUGUST 26, 1970

AD
MANIPULATION
UNITE FOR
WOMAN'S
EMANCIPATION

For 444 days, Iran held Americans—and America—hostage.

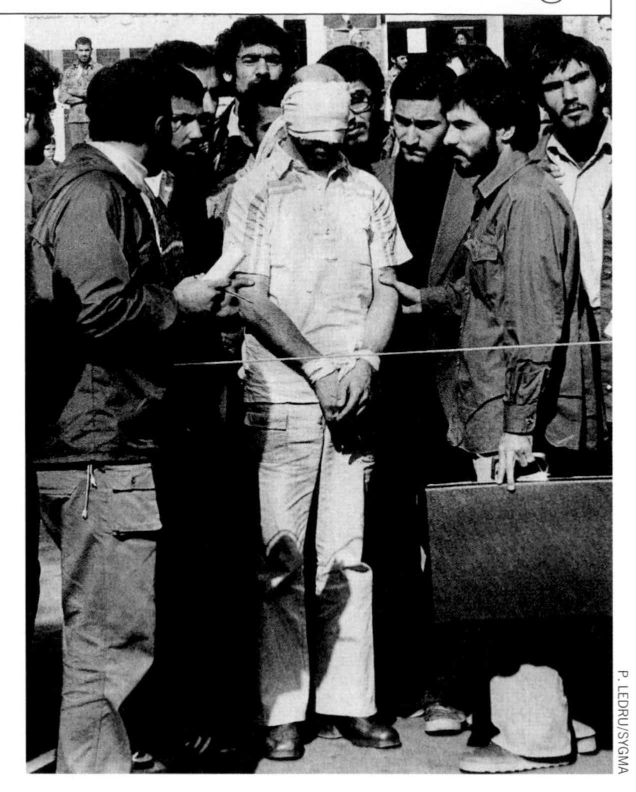

P. LEDRU/SYGMA

▲ AN EMBASSY HOSTAGE ON DISPLAY IN TEHRAN, NOVEMBER 1979

Accused of violating Islamic law, Mohammad Reza Pahlavi, the shah of Iran, was overthrown in 1979 by militant fundamentalists led by the Ayatollah Ruhollah Khomeini. In October the exiled shah—whose regime had been propped up by the United States since 1953—traveled to America for cancer treatments. On November 4 student revolutionaries seized the American embassy in Tehran, demanding that the shah be returned for trial. President Carter refused. The shah died July 27, 1980, but Iran did not free the 52 American hostages until January 20, 1981, the day Carter moved out of the White House.

P. LEDRU/SYGMA

▶ DEMONSTRATORS BURN AN EFFIGY OF UNCLE SAM, TEHRAN, NOVEMBER 1979

امام خمینی

In Beijing, peaceful protest turned violent; in L.A., violent protest upset a nation at peace.

ED CARREON/THE ORANGE COUNTY REGISTER/SIPA PRESS

▲ LOS ANGELES, APRIL 1992

One million people gathered in Beijing's Tiananmen Square (left) in the spring of 1989 and refused to leave. Their demand: democracy in China. On June 4 soldiers ended the seven-week vigil with a bloodbath, killing more than a thousand. During the protest, student leaders erected a crude replica of the Statue of Liberty, a symbol of the nation they hoped to emulate. Three years later the United States had its own problems with justice. Riots erupted in Los Angeles (above) after the acquittal of four white policemen caught on videotape beating a black man they had pulled over for speeding. More than 50 were killed. In Beijing protesters pleaded with soldiers: "We are people and you are people." In L.A., the beating victim, Rodney King, begged for an end to the violence, asking, "Can we all get along?"

STUART FRANKLIN/MAGNUM

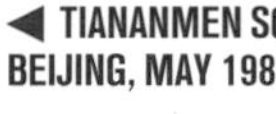

◀ TIANANMEN SQUARE, BEIJING, MAY 1989

FUNNY GIRL STAR BARBRA STREISAND 5/22/64

Arts & Entert

"Singing is almost like reading prose or poetry with a musical background. I think pop singing is a fine art form; **IT SHOULD MOVE PEOPLE LIKE A FINE PAINTING,** a fine piece of symphonic music or a fine acting job. People take it for granted because everybody sings."

—**FRANK SINATRA** LIFE, AUGUST 23, 1963

In 1964, Barbra Streisand (left) was the top female recording artist in the nation and, as the star of *Funny Girl,* a Broadway sensation. She was 22 years old. "I hadda be great," she told LIFE. "I couldn't be medium. My mouth was too big." Streisand is one of the many performers and artists LIFE has known who could never be considered *medium:* Among them are painters (Pablo Picasso, Henri Matisse), dancers (Martha Graham, Mikhail Baryshnikov), writers (Ernest Hemingway, Tennessee Williams), musicians (Louis Armstrong, Duke Ellington, Luciano Pavarotti, Frank Sinatra), comics (Lucille Ball, Bill Cosby), showmen (Bob Hope, Johnny Carson) and showwomen (Mary Martin, Julie Andrews). Not to mention the really, really big stars, talents who need no introductions—or surnames: Elvis, Madonna, John, Paul, George and Ringo.

ainment

BOB HOPE 1/10/44

MARY MARTIN IN *SOUTH PACIFIC* 4/18/49

JULIE ANDREWS IN *MY FAIR LADY* 3/26/56

GRANDMA MOSES TURNS 100 9/19/60

LOUIS ARMSTRONG 4/15/66

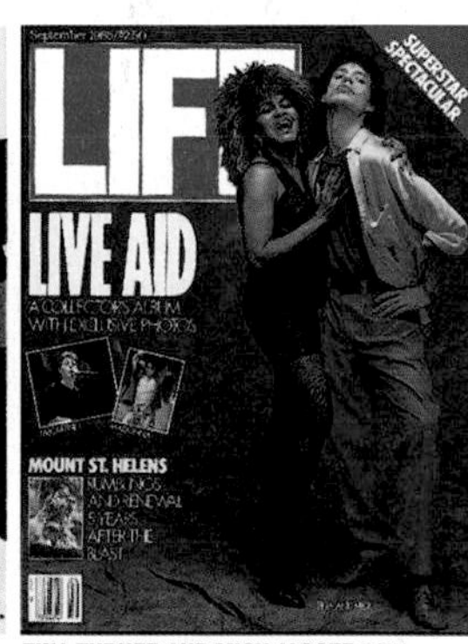

TINA TURNER AND MICK JAGGER 9/85

60

Martha Graham... Frank Sinatra... Duke Ellington... Ernest Hemingway

ROBERT CAPA

BARBARA MORGAN

HERBERT GEHR

GJON MILI

▲ FRANK SINATRA, 25, SINGING "AS TIME GOES BY," AT NEW YORK CITY'S CLUB RIOBAMBA, 1943

▲ ▲ MARTHA GRAHAM, 46, PICTURED IN 1940, 11 YEARS AFTER SHE HAD FORMED HER OWN DANCE COMPANY

In LIFE's first decade, Duke Ellington was revolutionizing jazz, Martha Graham was putting modern dance into motion, Frank Sinatra was a new (and to many men, inexplicable) heartthrob, and Ernest Hemingway was already a literary legend. Soon after *For Whom the Bell Tolls* was published in 1940, LIFE sent Hemingway's friend Robert Capa to photograph him "at work and play" in Sun Valley, Idaho. The master, 41, was seen writing while still in his pajamas (he penned his first drafts in longhand, working from six a.m. until two p.m.) and hunting pheasant at a neighbor's farm (opposite). Hemingway, LIFE wrote, was "a crack wing shot."

▲ DURING THIS 1943 JAM SESSION IN NEW YORK CITY, DUKE ELLINGTON, 44, PLAYED PAST FOUR A.M.

▶ ERNEST HEMINGWAY, 1941

Tennessee Williams...Martin & Lewis...Lucille Ball...Henri Matisse

ELIOT ELISOFON

▲ TENNESSEE WILLIAMS, 36, ON THE SET OF *STREETCAR,* BARRYMORE THEATRE, 1947

▼ "CRACKPOTS HIT JACKPOT," PROCLAIMED LIFE ABOUT COMEDY SENSATIONS DEAN MARTIN, 34, AND JERRY LEWIS, 25, ON TOUR IN 1951.

PHILIPPE HALSMAN

▶ "HER FINE FACE HAS BEEN BATTERED WITH PIES; HER STUNNING FIGURE HAS BEEN OBSCURED BY BAGGY-PANTS COSTUMES," SAID LIFE OF THE INDIGNITIES SUFFERED BY LUCILLE BALL (PICTURED IN 1950 AT AGE 39) FOR HER TV ALTER EGO, LUCY RICARDO.

PHILIPPE HALSMAN

Playwright Tennessee Williams, on the rise since 1945's *The Glass Menagerie,* shook up Broadway in 1947 with the provocative *A Streetcar Named Desire.* Four years later, in 1951, Dean Martin ("Sings with soggy languor," said LIFE) and Jerry Lewis ("Face like an orangutan") took to the road and became the highest-paid act in show business. Lucille Ball, a veteran of more than 50 films, conquered TV with *I Love Lucy,* which debuted on October 15. And Henri Matisse, who, at 81, had recently completed his work for the chapel in Vence, France, was honored with a traveling retrospective, which opened at New York's Museum of Modern Art.

DMITRI KESSEL

HENRI MATISSE,
AT HIS STUDIO IN
NICE, FRANCE, 1950

Elvis Presley ... Bob Dylan ... John, Paul, George & Ringo

TERENCE SPENCER

◀ WROTE LIFE IN 1964, WHEN THIS PHOTO FIRST APPEARED: "THE BEATLES? THEY ARE THE FOUR SHREWDLY GOOFY LOOKING LADS AT LEFT"—PAUL McCARTNEY, 21, GEORGE HARRISON, 21, JOHN LENNON, 23, AND RINGO STARR, 23.

▶ ABOUT ELVIS PRESLEY'S GYRATING HIPS (ON DISPLAY IN 1956), A 15-YEAR-OLD FAN SAID, "WHEN HE DOES THAT ON TV, I GET DOWN ON THE FLOOR AND SCREAM."

DAVID GAHR

▲ "MY RECORDS ARE SELLING AND I'M MAKING MONEY," SAID BOB DYLAN, 22 (PICTURED IN 1963), "BUT IT MAKES ME THINK I'M NOT DOING RIGHT."

Whether it was the southern boy who answered interviewers' questions with a "Yes, ma'am," four mop-tops from Liverpool or an intellectual folksinger from Minnesota, LIFE kept America's parents alerted to the dangerous characters from whom their kids might need protecting. "He uses a bump and grind routine usually seen only in burlesque," said LIFE of Elvis Presley, 21, in a 1956 article that showed churchgoers praying for his salvation. A week before the Beatles arrived in New York for their February 9, 1964, appearance on *The Ed Sullivan Show,* the magazine warned: "First England fell, victim of a million girlish screams. Then, last week, Paris surrendered. Now the U.S. must brace itself." And while LIFE did recognize Bob Dylan's folkie genius, it noted that he was "not exactly the image of the clean-cut boy you'd like your daughter to bring home to dinner."

CHARLES TRAINOR

ELVIS

Janis Joplin... Pablo Picasso... Mikhail Baryshnikov... Jimi Hendrix

In a 1968 issue devoted entirely to the most famous artist of the 20th century, the honoree, then 87, recollected: "When I was a child, my mother said to me, 'If you become a soldier, you'll be a general. If you become a monk, you'll end up as the pope.' Instead I became a painter and wound up as Picasso." The Spaniard's style, LIFE pointed out, was a precursor of the psychedelia in vogue in the late 1960s. In 1969, psychedelically inspired guitarist Jimi Hendrix told the magazine, "[Musicians] hypnotize people... [and] can preach into the subconscious what we want to say." (A year later both Hendrix and singer Janis Joplin were dead; she from a heroin overdose, he from drug-related asphyxiation.) But while modernism flourished, the classics still thrived. In 1974, Kirov star Mikhail Baryshnikov defected to the U.S.—and leapt into the spotlight as America's most celebrated ballet dancer.

◀ JANIS JOPLIN, 25, AT THE NEWPORT FOLK FESTIVAL, 1968

DAVID GAHR

EDWARD QUINN/GAMMA LIAISON

▲ PABLO PICASSO, WITH HIS WIFE AND FREQUENT MODEL, JACQUELINE, IN 1968

▶ MIKHAIL BARYSHNIKOV, 27, IN 1975

© MAX WALDMAN ARCHIVES

◀ AT THE MONTEREY POP FESTIVAL IN 1967, JIMI HENDRIX, 24, SET HIS GUITAR ON FIRE.

ED CARAEFF

Bill Cosby . . . Luciano Pavarotti

MICHAEL O'BRIEN

▲ BILL COSBY (AND DOUBLE), 1985

Two virtuosos—one of opera, one of comedy—both adored by audiences. In 1980, LIFE visited Luciano Pavarotti—"the world's busiest tenor"—while he summered at home in Italy. He had just completed a grueling spring season of 85 performances around the world and was about to begin rigorous rehearsals for New York's Metropolitan Opera. "The attention is like a drug to him," his wife, Adua, commented. "He likes to feel grand." (The Pavarottis have since separated.) Five years later the magazine hooked up with entertainer Bill Cosby, 47, as he met fans of his hit sitcom, *The Cosby Show.* "Hi, Bill, I really, really love your show," admirers kept hollering. And the man TV viewers knew as Cliff Huxtable, a doctor and funny father of five, answered, "And I really love doing it for you."

MIRELLA RICCIARDI/GAMMA LIAISON

▶ LUCIANO PAVAROTTI, 45, AT HOME IN MODENA, ITALY, IN 1980 WITH (FROM LEFT) HIS WIFE, ADUA, AND DAUGHTERS LORENZA, GIULIANA AND CHRISTINA

HARRY BENSON (2)

Johnny... Dave... Dolly... Madonna... Michael [and Lisa Marie]

▶ *LATE NIGHT'S* DAVID LETTERMAN, 39, IN 1986, HOST OF WHAT LIFE CALLED A "MAD, MAD, MAD, MAD TALK SHOW"

THEO WESTENBERGER

▶▶ IN 1995, LISA MARIE PRESLEY, 27, AND MICHAEL JACKSON, 36, POSED FOR LIFE IN CELEBRATION OF THEIR FIRST (AND, IT WOULD TURN OUT, ONLY) WEDDING ANNIVERSARY.

▶ SAID DOLLY PARTON, 40 (PHOTOGRAPHED IN 1986): "I'VE RELIED ON DOLLY'S IMAGE TO CARRY ME A LONG WAY."

ENRICO FERORELLI

BRUCE WEBER

▶▶ WROTE LIFE ABOUT MADONNA, 28, IN 1986: "[SHE] EXUDES OLD-STYLE HOLLYWOOD EXCITEMENT LIKE NO OTHER ENTERTAINER TODAY."

◀ ON MAY 22, 1992, HAVING DELIVERED HIS 4,531ST *TONIGHT SHOW* MONOLOGUE, JOHNNY CARSON, 66, SAID GOOD NIGHT—AND GOODBYE.

After 30 years as the king of late-night TV, Johnny Carson called it quits. Among the iconic entertainers of the late '80s and early '90s who never strayed too far from the spotlight: David Letterman, who, with great fanfare, moved his talk show from NBC to CBS in 1993; Dolly Parton, the country music superstar, sometime actress and theme park proprietor; Madonna, the regularly reinvented pop singer, sometime actress and savvy self-promoter; and Michael Jackson, the most famous (and often infamous) entertainer in the world, whose phenomenal success ranks right up there with that of the Beatles (whose songs he co-owns) and Elvis Presley (whose daughter he married).

Nature's

JAPANESE MACAQUE 1/30/70

"Immersion in wilderness life, like immersion in the sea, **MAY RETURN CIVILIZED MAN** to a basic element from which he sprang and with which he has now lost contact."

—ANNE MORROW LINDBERGH, WRITING ABOUT BEING ON SAFARI IN EAST AFRICA LIFE, OCTOBER 21, 1966

Wonders

OLD FAITHFUL 8/19/46

UTAH'S ARCHES 4/13/53

QUEEN TRIGGERFISH 11/30/53

BRAZILIAN JAGUAR 3/16/59

ALL ABOUT TREES 5/90

AMERICA'S PARKS, SUMMER 1991

The first animal to rate its own story in the Bible was the serpent in Eden. In LIFE, that honor belongs to the similarly dangerous black widow spider. From the magazine's debut issue, November 23, 1936: "Comes, too, a lover, a male . . . who knows that chances are the lady won't like him. [She] leaves him sucked dry and bloodless—a withered brittle corpse, solemnly enshrouded by his hungry wife." The sensationalism of LIFE's nature reporting has toned down a bit over the years, but not the magazine's curiosity about all the wonders of Earth—the wild beasts and birds, the seascapes and deserts, the mountains and meadows. In 1991, in a celebration of America's national parks, essayist Edward Hoagland wrote in LIFE, "Children need a world with more animals than Kermit the Frog and Big Bird." And they need flowers, trees and fresh air, beautiful sunsets and sunrises.

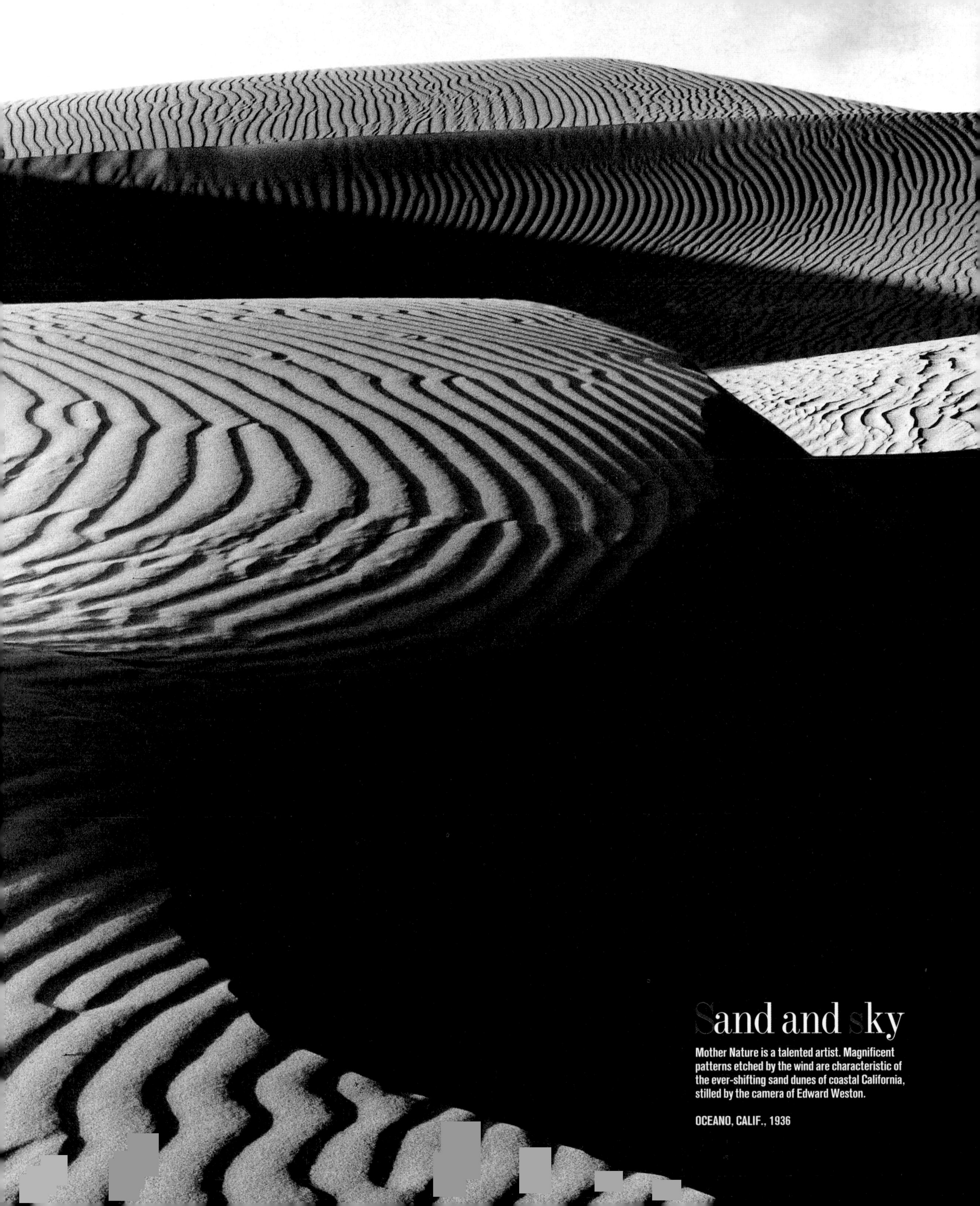

Sand and sky

Mother Nature is a talented artist. Magnificent patterns etched by the wind are characteristic of the ever-shifting sand dunes of coastal California, stilled by the camera of Edward Weston.

OCEANO, CALIF., 1936

DMITRI KESSEL

Mountains and valleys

The mist-veiled hills of the Yangtze river valley have appeared in Chinese art for centuries. "Veneration of nature is a theme that pervades Chinese religion," wrote LIFE in the story about Confucianism in which this photograph, taken by Dmitri Kessel during a seven-month assignment in China, first appeared. Paintings and photos are all that will remain of this landscape after the Three Gorges Dam, scheduled for completion in 2009, floods some 350 miles of the river canyon, destroying temples, rock carvings and the homes of more than one million people.

WUSHAN GORGE, CHINA, 1946

Wind and waves

"Man can make the desert bloom . . . [but] he can never conquer the implacable sea," wrote LIFE to introduce Leonard McCombe's photo-essay about oceans, for which he logged 63,000 miles over six months. He saw the calm of Bahamian shallows, the teeming marine life of Peru's coast and, here, the tumultuous crash of a New England nor'easter.

NEAR THE THACHER'S ISLAND LIGHTHOUSE, CAPE ANN, MASS., 1962

LEONARD MCCOMBE

Hunter and prey

For eight months LIFE photographer John Dominis stalked the wild cats of Africa—including the leopard, described by the magazine as "the shrewdest, the loneliest, the most patient and the most vicious of the great cats." Demonstrating those qualities, a male leopard stationed himself in a tree to devour his kill, an 80-pound springbok.

BOTSWANA, AFRICA, 1966

JOHN DOMINIS

HARALD SUND

Water and stone

For decades, a thirsty Los Angeles has tapped the rivers that feed Mono Lake, located just east of Yosemite. The water level of the 100-square-mile lake has dropped precipitously (more than 40 feet during the past half century), uncovering these Ice Age stalagmites—limestone turrets, actually. In the 1980s, area residents, alarmed by the continuing ecological damage, lobbied for limits on the amount of water that could be pumped to L.A. The flow south has since been slowed.

Trees and Flowers

America's National Park Service celebrated its 75th anniversary in 1991. Seventy-two years earlier, Acadia had become the first national park east of the Mississippi. Located on Maine's Mount Desert Island, it is a jewel box of granite, kelly green lichens and scarlet foliage.

ACADIA NATIONAL PARK, MAINE, 1990

CARR CLIFTON

Sleeping Beauty

"I am all alone, just looking and looking." The words are Teiji Saga's, whose passion for three decades was taking pictures of swans. But the statement could have been made by any of the thousands of photographers whose work has appeared in LIFE. Men and women whose dedication to the art of looking—and seeing—has enriched us all.

HOKKAIDO, JAPAN, 1974

TEIJI SAGA/PACIFIC PRESS SERVICE/PHOTO RESEARCHERS